Memori~ Norton G~~en

The first village on the River Trent

VIEW OF NORTON GREEN HALL.
near the Staffordshire Potteries.

View of Norton Green Hall 1842. Built around 1650.

Compiled by
The Norton Green History Group

Acknowledgments

Norton Green History Group would like to express its most sincere thanks to the following parties for their help in making this publication possible.

All of our oral and photographic contributors from our community.
Members of our community who have worked tirelessly on this project.
Stafford Record Office Archives.
Stoke-on-Trent City Library Archives
The Old Nortonian Society.
Leek Post and Times
Scholastic Souvenirs, Blackpool.
Staffordshire Sentinel Newspapers.
The National Lottery 'Awards For All' (for their funding of this project)

CONTENTS

NORTON.

NORTON is a village and parish, about 2½ miles N.E. by E. of Burslem, and 4 from Stoke-upon-Trent.

POST OFFICE :—

Mr. Joseph Ball, postmaster. Letters arrive and are despatched viâ Stoke. Delivery commences at 7-15 a.m. Box closes for despatch of letters at 6-10 p.m. On Sundays at 1-10 p.m. Nearest Money Order Office, Burslem.

PUBLIC OFFICERS, &c. :—

Assistant Overseer—Mr. Samuel Billinge.
Collector of Poor Rates—Mr. Samuel Billinge.
County Court—Norton is in the Hanley District, which see for Officers, &c.
Police Constable—Mr. Howard Betts.
Registrar of Births and Deaths—Mr. John Salt, Endon, comes over every Saturday.

PLACES OF WORSHIP :—

St. Bartholomew's—Rev. John Anderson, M.A., Rector.
Primitive Methodist Chapel and at Chell Heath.
Wesleyan Chapel.

PUBLIC SCHOOL :—St. Bartholomew (National)—Mr. Day, Master ; Mrs. Unwin, Mistress ; Miss Ann Holdcroft, Infants' Mistress.

CONVEYANCE :—The Ford Green Station of the North Staffordshire Railway, for passengers and goods, is about 1 mile from Norton.

1869–70

Alcock John, butcher
Anderson Rev. J., M.A., rector of St. Luke's
Ball Joseph, grocer and draper
Barker & Cope, ironfounders, Norton green
Bennett William, Fir tree farm
Billinge Samuel, collector of rates [green
Cartledge John, wheelwright, Baddeley
Clews John, clogger
Cope Joseph, mining engineer
Cope William, surveyor
Cope Mrs., Norton green
Cope Thomas, Holden bridge brickyards
Cope Thomas, wheelwright, Ball green
Critchlow Bernard, grocer,&c.,Norton grn.
Dale Wm., Chell heath, smallware dealer
Day William, National schoolmaster
Dean John, farmer, Heakley farm
Dean Josiah, farmer, Greenway bank
Dean Richard, Spragg house
Emberton Isaac, farmer, Dog croft
Edward Andrew, manager Whitfield Colliery Company
Ferneyhough Thomas, brickmaker
Frost William, forge manager
Fynney John, corn miller, Whitfield mills
Heath Robert, ironmaster and coal proprietor, Biddulph valley colliery
Heath Wm., gentleman, Dog croft
Holdcroft George, bootmaker, Ball green
Holdcroft Ralph, farmer, Smallthorne
Houldcroft Daniel, farmer, Ball green
Houldcroft John, farmer, Ball green
Houldcroft Ralph, blacksmith, Ball green
Houldcroft Richd., bootmaker, Ball green
Houldcroft Sarah, beerseller, Ball green
Houldcroft Wm., blacksmith, Ball green
Irving Robert, *Bell and Dragon*
Jenks George, grocer, &c., Norton green
Johnson Simeon, road surveyor, Norton gn.
Kent James, joiner and wheelwright, Norton green
Lambsdale Richard beer retailer Norton green
Latham John, shopkeeper, Chell heath
Latham John, Catherine field farm
Leak Hamlet, whitesmith
Leak Martin, general smith, New Inn bank
Lovatt John, *Robin Hood & Little John* New Inn bank
Mayer George, coal dealer
Mayer Elijah, beerseller, Norton green
Mayer John, shopkeeper, Norton green
Mayer Mary, *Duke of Wellington Inn*
Morris John M., surgeon
Mosedale Sarah, dressmaker
Mould Enoch, clogger, North green
Mountford Josh., tailor
Mountford Elijah, parish clerk & sexton
Mountford Samuel, Ford green farm
Palmer Stephen, surgeon
Palin W., cashier for R. Heath, Esq.
Pointon Henry, butcher
Redfern John, Heathfields
Sargeant John, farmer, Ball green
Scragg Hugh, farmer
Scragg Samuel, builder
Scragg Samuel, grocer, &c., Norton, and draper at Dog croft
Shaw Charles A., surgeon
Shufflebotham Chas. S., Dog croft farm
Smith Thos., farmer, New ford, Norton
Stevenson Robert, saddler
Sutton Richard, farmer, Whitfield
Taylor Thomas, blacksmith
Tomkinson Samuel, *Cock Inn*
Turner Samuel, farmer, Norton green farm
Turner Thomas, farmer, Adam's croft
Unwin Mrs. Mary, cowkeeper
Unwin James, Bradley, Smallthorne
Unwin Susannah, mistress National school
Walker George, farmer, Norton green
Walker Peter, grocer and draper
Whitfield Colliery Company Norton-in-the Moors
Wood Ralph, beerseller, Ball green
Wright John, hardware dealer

NORTON-IN-THE-MOORS is a parish, township and extensive moorland district, 1 mile from Milton station on the Leek branch and 1 mile from Ford Green and Smallthorne station on the Biddulph branch of the North Staffordshire railway, and extending from 3 to 4 miles east-north-east from Burslem, and within 6 south-west of Leek, in the Leek division of the county, hundred and petty sessional division of Pirehill North, union of Leek, county court district of Burslem, rural deanery of Leek, archdeaconry of Stoke-on-Trent, and diocese of Lichfield. The Cauldon canal passes through. The church of St. Bartholomew, rebuilt in 1738, is a plain structure of brick, consisting of chancel with vestry, nave of three bays, aisles and a western tower, containing 6 fine-toned bells, cast by William Dobson, of Downham, Norfolk, in 1826: the chancel was rebuilt in 1899 and the church was enlarged in 1914, at a cost of £2,500, from designs by Mr. J. H. Beckett A.R.I.B.A. of Longton: there are sittings for 420 persons. The registers date from 1537. The living is a rectory, net yearly value £450, with residence, erected in 1826 by the Rev. G. B. Wilding, and rebuilt in 1875, in the gift of Lord Norton, and held since 1921 by the Rev. John George Hamlet B.A. of London University. There is a Wesleyan chapel in the village and one at Stockton Brook, erected in 1909, with 200 sittings, a' Primitive Methodist chapel at Norton Green, and a United Methodist chapel at Ball Green. The general charities amount to about £6 yearly. There are various collieries in the neighbourhood, and iron works at Ford Green. At Greenway Bank is the beautiful residence of Robert William Heath esq. J.P. Lord Norton and Sir George Guy Chetwynd bart. are joint lords of the manor and the two principal landowners. The soil is strong and heavy; subsoil, clay. The chief crops are wheat, oats and turnips. The parish comprises the hamlets of Bemmersley, the villages of Norton Green, Ball Green, Baddeley Green. Milton is now a separate parish, and Smallthorne an Urban District. The area is 3,412 acres of land and 37 of water; rateable value, £26,040; the population of the civil parish in 1911 was 5,299, and of the ecclesiastical parish, 3,000.

Post, M. O., T. & Telephone Call Office, Norton.—Mrs. Edith Ann Parton, sub-postmistress. Letters from Stoke-on-Trent arrive by messenger from Smallthorne. Telegrams are dispatched from this office, but Smallthorne is the nearest telegraph office, 2½ miles distant, for delivery

Wall Pillar Box, Norton Green

BEMMERSLEY hamlet, in the north of the parish, is in the union of Leek, near Black Bull (Childerplay) station on the Biddulph branch.

Parish Clerk, William Repton.

Public Elementary Schools.

Norton, built in 1797 & enlarged 1848 & 1880-4, for 133 boys, 88 girls & 72 infants; Joseph E. Rhodes, master; Miss Harriett Hinchco, mistress; Mrs. Ethel Ford, infants' mistress; the schools have been liberally endowed by the late Miss Sparrow

Norton Green (mixed & infants), built in 1879, for 164 boys & girls & 129 infants; Moses Fereday, master

Baddeley Green, built in 1912, for 200 mixed & 100 infants; Joel Southworth, master; Miss Ruth Walley, infants' mistress

Baddeley Edge, Ball Green and Baddeley Green are hamlets in the parish.

PRIVATE RESIDENTS.

(Marked thus * receive letters through Stockton Brook.)

Brookes Frederick George, Spragg ho
Davenport John Aldersey M.B., Ch.B. Ford Green house
Deane William Poole, Hargreaves cot
Glass Charles Stanley, Hillside
Glover Thomas E. 56 Leek road
Hamlet Rev. John George B.A L.C.P. (rector)
Harding Roland Charles, Old Rectory
Hartland Harry, Manor house
Harvey William, Whitfield
Heath Robt.Wm. J.P. Greenway bank
*Matthews Isaac J.P. Lawton house, Nursery road, Baddeley Green
Mayer John Thomas, Bemmersley (letters through Brindley Ford)
Pickford Ernest, New hall
Smith Percy Wm. Thos. Norton hall
Smith Robert, Highfield (letters through Brindley Ford)
Wain Edward B. Whitfield
Wood Charles, Mount Pleasant

COMMERCIAL.

Adams Elizh.(Mrs.))Norton Arms P.H
*Adams Stephen, shopkeeper, 48 Victoria street, Baddeley Green
*Baddeley Green Working Men's Club & Institute, Leek road
*Bailey Charles, shopkeeper, 115 Leek road, Baddeley Green
Bailey John, farmer, Greenway bank
*Baker Beatrice (Mrs.), draper, Leek road, Baddeley Green
Baker Walter, cycle dlr. 7 High st
Ball Frederick William, farmer
Bamford John Willott, assistant overseer, Norton Green
Bamford William, picture frame maker, Norton Green
*Baskeyfield William George, police sergeant, Baddeley Green
Beardmore Emma (Mrs.), milliner, Norton Green
Berrisford Henry, butcher

Berrisford John Wm. frmr. Ball Grn
Berrisford Saml. farmr. Yew Tree fm
*Beswick George Thomas, farmer, Baddeley Hall farm
Boulton Joseph, farmr. Foundry farm
Brammer Douglas,frmr.Baddeley edge
*Brookes Arthur, shopkeeper, 32 Victoria street, Baddeley Green
Burslem & District Industrial Cocperative Society Limited
*Byrne James, hair dresser, Leek rd.
Carp Horatio Nelson, frmr. Ball frm
*Cartlidge John, hawker, Leek road, Baddeley Green
Chadwick Hugh, shpkpr.Whitfield rd
Chatterley-Whitfield Collieries Ltd
Clarkson Edgar, farmer, Annatt's ho. High lane
Clay Faith Winifred (Miss), midwife, 12 Mount Pleasant
Clowes Chas. Edwin, Robin Hood P.H
Clowes John Jas. grocr.Norton Green
*Dale Ephraim, grocer, Leek road, Baddeley Green
*Dale John, clogger, 123 Leek road, Baddeley Green
Dale Jsph. grocr.Norton-in-the-Moors
Dale Samuel, baker, 17 High street
Davenport John Aldersey M.B., Ch.B. physician & surgeon, & medical officer of health to the Smallthorne Urban District Council, Ford Green house
Dawson Elizabeth (Miss), district nurse, Providence cottage
Dawson Violet(Mrs.),shpkpr.3 Cornhill
Deane William Poole, architect, Hargreaves cottage
Forrester Peter, beer retlr.Ball Green
Fox Albert, boot maker, High street
Fryer Charles, shopkpr. Norton Green
Gerrard David Machen,frmr.Whitfield
Glass Charles Stanley M.B., Ch.B. physician & surgeon, & medical officer & public vaccinator to Leek union, Hillside
Goodwin Arthur,farmr.Bank End frm

Griffiths Edward John, Duke of Wellington P.H
Grime Joseph, shopkpr. 28 Ridgeway
Hackney George, corn dealer, Bemmersley (letters through Brindley Ford)
*Hammond Edwin, shopkeeper, 10 Victoria street, Baddeley Green
Harvey John Ryder, farmer,Whitfield
Harvey Joseph, farmer, Whitfield mill
Harvey Samuel, farmer, Heakley
Hawley Charles James, hair dresser
Heath Robert & Lowmoor Limited, coal & iron masters, Norton collieries & iron works
Heath Samuel, farmer, Norton Green
Holdcroft John James, shopkeeper, 31 North street, Ball Green
Holdcroft Thomas, farmer, Ball Green
*Holland Herbert, shopkeeper, 83 Leek road, Baddeley Green
Hulme Henry, shopkeeper, Cornhill
*Hurd Arthur, grocer, & post office, Leek road, Baddeley Green
*James H. & Sons, butchers, Leek rd. Baddeley Green
*James Henry, frmr. Baddeley Grn
Johnson William, news agt. Cornhill
Jolley Jesse, shopkeepr.Norton Green
Jolley Mary (Miss), milliner, 22 Orchard croft
Jones John, smallholder, Oldhall
Kirkham Thomas L. & John William, coal dealers, 4 Cornhill
Machin James William, farmer
*Matthews Arthur Percival, nurseryman, Highfield nurseries, Baddeley Green
Mayer Arthur, beer retlr. Ball Green
Mayer Jas. beer retailer, Norton Grn
Mayer John, boot maker, Norton Grn
Meakin Mary Ellen (Mrs.), grocer, Norton Green
Morris John, beer retlr.Norton Green
Morris Mary Lucy (Mrs.), shopkeeper, North street, Ball Green
Mottram Joseph, grocer, 104 Leek rd
Mottram Thomas, earthenware dealer, 106 Leek road

COMMERCIAL CONT'D

Parton Joseph Hy. stationer, Leek rd
*Patrick Henry Rock, draper, 46 Victoria street, Baddeley Green
Pegg Bertram, shopkeeper, Cornhill
Pointon William, stationer, & post office, North street, Ball Green
Rogers Joseph, coal dealer
*Rogers Walt. coal mer.Baddeley Grn
Ryles George J. grocer
Sargeant Richard, shopkpr. Ball Grn
Sheldon Albert E. grocer, Norton Grn
Sheldon Sampson,shopkpr.Foundry sq
Sherratt Saml. farmer, Norton Green

*Simmons Ambrose, shopkeeper, 73 Leek road, Baddeley Green
Smith Percy William Thomas,farmer, Norton hall
Tatton Benjamin, farmer,Bemmersley (letters through Brindley Ford)
Tatton William, farmer, Bemmersley (letters through Brindley Ford)
Taylor John, blacksmith
*Taylor Wm. beer retlr.Baddeley Grn
Taylor William Cecil, hardware dlr. 44 Leek road
Thompson Thos. shopkeeper.Whitfield rd

Thursfield Frederick William, farmer
Triner Edward, saddler, 2 High st
Walker Allen, shopkeeper, 12 High st
Walker Edward John, grocer, High st
Walker George Wood, registrar of births & deaths & relieving officer & vaccination officer, Norton Green
Wilshaw Wm. farmer, Baddeley Grn
Winkle Enoch, frmr.Ridgway Hall fm
Working Men's Club & Institute Ltd. (William Pointon, sec)
Wright Albt. shopkpr. Norton Green

(Marked thus * receive letters through Stockton Brook, Stoke.)

PRIVATE RESIDENTS.

(For T N's see general list of Private Residents at end of book.)

Allman A., Spragg house
Boulton A. Manor house
Croft Herbert J. Whitfield
Davenport John Aldersey M.B., Ch.B. Ford Green house
Deane William Poole, Hargreaves cot
Glass Charles Starley, Hillside
Hamlet Rev. John George B.A., L.C.P. (rector)
Harvey David, Whitfield

COMMERCIAL CONTD

Billinge D. & E. shopkpr. High st
Blackhurst Abraham, cowkpr. 41 North st. Ball Green
*Boulton Albt. grocer, 115 Leek rd. Baddeley Green
Boulton Arth. farmer, Foundry farm
*Boulton Ernest. boot repr. 99 Leek rd. Baddeley Green
Boulton Herbt. High Street farm
*Boulton Mrs. Mary A. shopkpr. 12 Victoria st. Baddeley Green
Boulton Thos. beer retlr. New inn, Ball Green
Brammer Douglas, farmer, Baddeley edge (postal address, Milton)
Bratt Arth. butcher, Whitfield rd
Breeze Zillah (Mrs.), grocer, Norton Green
*Brookes Arthur, shopkeeper, 32 Victoria street, Baddeley Green
Brown Enoch, farmer, Yew Tree frm
Burslem & District Industrial Co-operative Society Ltd. High street
*Byrne Jas. hairdrssr. 129 Leek rd. Baddeley Green
Cantrell Geo. smallholder, Low. Flatt farm, Norton Green
*Cartlidge John, hawker, Leek road, Baddeley Green
Chadwick Hugh,grocer,23 Whitfield rd
*Charlesworth Thos. farmer, Red Lime farm, Baddeley Edge
Chatterley-Whitfield Collieries Ltd. T N's Hanley 7184 & 7185
City Window Cleaners, Tunsball & Ball Green
Clarke Chas. shopkpr. 31 North st. Ball Green
Clay Faith Winifred (Miss), midwife, 12 Mount Pleasant
Corbishley Hy. farmer, Norton Green
Clowes John Jas. grocr.Norton Green
Crump Jn. Norton Arms P.H
*Dale Jn. grocer, 125 Leek rd. Baddeley Green
Dale Jsph. grocer
Dale Samuel, baker, 17 High street
Davenport Jn. Aldersey M.B., Ch.B. physcn. & surgn. Ford Green. T N Hanley 7616
Dawson Lawrence, newsagt. Leek rd. Baddeley Green
Dawson Violet(Mrs.),shpkpr.3 Cornhill
Deane William Poole, architect, Hargreaves cottage
District Nurses' Home, High st
Eardley Wm. hairdrssr. Leek rd. Baddeley Green
*Finikin Wm. insur. agt. 4 Victoria st. Baddeley Green
Fox Albert, boot maker, High street
Gerrard David Machen,frmr.Whitfield
Glass Charles Stanley M.B., Ch.B physician & surgeon, & medical officer & public vaccinator, Hillside. T N Hanley 7656
Glover Percy, farmer, Chapel la. Baddeley Edge
Goodwin Arthur,farmr.Bank End frm
Goodwin Geo. H. beer retlr. Norton Green

Heath Robert William M.A., J.P. Greenway bank
Jack James, 56 Leek road
Maskery Herbert, Highfield, Bemmersley (letters through Brindley Ford)
Mayer John Thomas, Bemmersley (letters through Brindley Ford)
Moreton John, 20 Orchard croft
Wilson Thomas M., M.B., Ch.B. Old Rectory
Winkle Hugh, Norton Green hall

COMMERCIAL.

*Adams Jas. painter, 89 Leek rd. Baddeley Green
Gratton Eleanor (Mrs.), farmer, Ridgway Hall farm
Gratton Thos. A. painter, Whitfield rd
Griffiths Harriett (Mrs.), Duke of Wellngton P.H
Hackney George, corn dealer, Bemmersley (letters through Brindley Ford)
Hall Harriett (Mrs.), shopkpr. 1 Ridgway
Hampson & Burnham, electrcl. engnrs. Whitfield rd
Hampson Arth. confctnr. 93 Leek rd. Baddeley Green
*Hammond Edwin, shopkpr. 10 Victoria st. Baddeley Green
Hardy Thos. hairdrssr. Leek rd
Hargreaves Ann B. (Mrs.), statnr. & postmaster, Ball Green
Harvey David, farmer, Fir Tree farm & Whitfield Mill farm
Harvey Geo. farmer, Norton hall
Hassel Wm. farmer, Annatt's House farm, High la
*Hawley Elijah, assistant insur. supt. Feandale, Baddeley Green
Hayes Edith (Mrs.), confctnr. Baddeley Edge
Holdcroft Fredk. farmer, Ball Green
Holdcroft Geo. H. shopkpr. Ball Grn
Holdcroft Jn. nurseryman, Glen Brae, Ball Green
Howard J. & Son, haulage contrctrs
*Hulme Rachel (Mrs.), shopkpr. 51 Victoria st. Baddeley Green
*Hurd Ellen (Mrs.), grocer, & post office, Leek rd. Baddeley Green
*James H. & Sons, butchers, Leek rd. Baddeley Green
*James Harry, farmer, Baddeley Grn
*James Hy. farmer, Baddeley Green. T N Endon 50
*James Sarah (Mrs.), grocer, 48 Victoria st. Baddeley Green
Johnson William, news agt. Cornhill
Johnson Geo. H. Robin Hood P.H
Jolley Jesse, shopkeepr.Norton Green
Jolley Jesse, beer retlr. Norton Green
Jolley Mary (Miss), milliner, 22 Orchard croft
Knight Josiah & Sons, haulage contrctrs. 56 Whitfield rd
Lear Sarah A. (Mrs.), greengro. 5 High st. Cornhill
Lowe Arth. insur. agt. Cornhill
Lowe Ernest, shpkpr.33 Whitfield rd
Lowe Mary (Mrs.), grocer, Cornhill
Maddock Edwin, hairdrssr. 59 High st
Mather Mary (Miss) shopkpr. Norton Green
*Matthews Arthur Percival, nurseryman, Highfield nurseries, Baddeley Green. T N Endon 40
Mayer Bros. haulage contrctrs. Bemmersley (postal address, Brindley Ford). T N Biddulph 34
Mayer Elijah, farmer, Up. Heakley farm, Ball la
*Mayer Jas. garage, Leek rd. Baddeley Green. T N Endon 76

*Baddeley Green Motor Repair Depot, Leek rd. Baddeley Green. T N Endon 83
*Baddeley Green Working Men's Club & Institute (Albt. Boulton, sec.), Leek rd. Baddeley Green
Bailey Jn. farmer, Greenway bank (postal address, Brindley Ford)
Ball Fredk. Wm. farmer, Heakley frm
Ball Green Working Men's Club & Institute Ltd. (Reg. Holdcroft, sec.), North st. Ball Green
Berrisford Hy. butcher, High st
Berrisford Hy. frmr. Ball Green frm
*Beswick George Thomas. farmer, Baddeley Hall farm
Mountford Jn. shopkpr. 65 North st. Ball Green
*Mountford Margt. (Mrs.) C.M.B. midwife, Penarth, Baddeley Green. T N Endon 10
*Neild T. hairdrssr. Leek rd. Baddeley Green
Norton & Biddulph Collieries Ltd. coal masters, Norton collieries. T N Hanley 7155
Norton Garage Co. Leek rd. T N Hanley 7614
Oakes Wm. shopkpr. 28 Ridgeway
Rogers Joseph, coal dlr.Norton Green
*Rogers W. & Co. coal mers. Baddeley Green
Ryles George J. grocer
Sandbach Alfd. R., M.P.S. chemist, High st
Sargeant Arron, beer retlr. Ball Grn
Sheldon Albt. E. coal dlr. Norton Green
Sheldon Thos. Leek rd. Norton Green
Sherratt Sarah (Mrs.), farmer, Norton Green
Sherratt Wm. A. farmer, Church frm
Sillito Doris(Miss) A.L.C.M.,L.L.C.M. teacher of music, Melvedor
*Simmons Ambrose, shopkeeper, 73 Leek road, Baddeley Green
Staffordshire Potteries Water Board Pumping Station, Stockton Brook. T N Endon 17
Stanley Hena (Mrs.), shopkpr. Whitfield rd
Stringer Jsph. bldr. Baddeley Green. T N Endon 84
Stubbs Jn. E. farmer, Yew Tree farm, Norton Green
Tatton Lei, farmer, Bemmersley (letters through Brindley Ford)
Tatton William, farmer, Bemmersley (letters through Brindley Ford)
Taylor Wm blacksmith
*Taylor Wm. beer retlr. Victoria inn, Baddeley Green
Taylor Wm. C. ironmngr. High st. T N Hanley 8321
Thompson Thos. shopkpr. 165 Whitfield rd
Thursfield Frederick William, farmer
Trickett Saml. farmr. Ford Green fm
Triner Edward, saddler, 2 High st
Triner Hannah (Mrs.), shopkpr. 7 High st
Turner Gladys (Mrs.), confctnr. 103 North st. Ball Green
Turner Phoebe (Mrs.), farmer, Ball Lane cott
Walker Allen, shopkeeper, 12 High st
Webb Beatrice (Mrs.), grocer, 104 Leek rd. Norton Green
Wilson Harry, fried fish dlr. Whitfield rd
Wilson Thos. M., M.B., Ch.B. physcn. & surgn. Old Rectory. T N Hanley 8231
Working Men's Club & Institute Ltd. (Frank Morris, sec)
Yardley Rd. clogger, Norton Green
Y.M.C.A. (Arth. Rhodes, sec.),High st

INTRODUCTION

During the summer of 2006 Norton Green Residents Association formed a History Group to explore and research the history and heritage of our village.

It was decided that our first project would be an oral history publication to record the memories of residents of this village during the 20th century.

As the project developed we realised that within each story there were references made to significant historical events, sights or buildings. We therefore thought it appropriate to research certain subjects and add them between the chapters of this book.

We do not declare this publication to be a definitive history or account of our village but a collection of memories as told by residents together with some researched articles by Norton Green History Group (NGHG).

A view of Leek Road around the turn of the 20th century.

Alan Holdcroft - Hog roast

As a young boy growing up in Norton Green around the late 1950s and 60s I used to collect waste food from around the village on a Sunday afternoon. People used to save up their vegetable peelings, bread etc for me to collect with my little two wheeled cart and sack bags. I would take the waste to Reg Simpson at Old Hall Farm to feed his pigs. We would empty the contents of the sacks into a big cast iron pot and light a fire underneath it to boil it up.

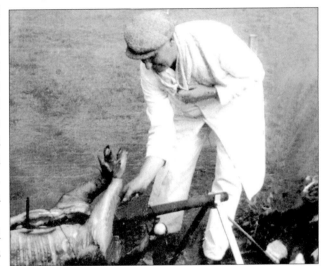

The next day, when it had cooled down we would feed it to his pigs and I was given a shilling for the job.

Another childhood memory I have is the Village Hog Roast. Ernie Travis, the local butcher, would call for me early one morning and we would go down to the Tank field where Ernie and Sam Hancock would dig a pit out and light a fire in it. There they would proceed to roast a pig on a spit that Ernie had donated.

The pig was roasted all day, and meanwhile a big white marquee was erected and tables and chairs brought inside. At night the pig was taken into the marquee and sliced up to make sandwiches which were sold.

Sam Hancock basting the pig.

I think they also had a supply of beer because I remember putting my head under the Marquee at night and being told to 'get out!' I was there all day and never even got a sandwich.

Reg Simpson from Old Hall Farm delivering fruit and veg by horse and cart.

Front row from left Ernie Travis, Dick Holdcroft and Sam Hancock at the hog roast on the Tank field.

Gathering around the hog roast in the 1950s.

Alex Hancock - A landlord's memories of the Foaming Quart

I was born in Cobridge and lived there for a couple of years until my family moved to Norton Green. One of my earliest memories of living in Norton Green was that the men of the village, every Sunday, would play 'shotties' (marbles) against the wall of Boulton's farm on Foundry Square. They'd take a brush and sweep a spot clean and play 'Chink' for pennies; this was grown men not kids!

As a child I can remember going 'pig-nutting' in Mr Corbishley's fields at Backfold Farm. Pig-nuts grew under the ground and you had to dig them up and I don't think Mr Corbishley liked us kids doing that! I don't think anybody goes 'pig-nutting' nowadays.

Living in the village my father Frederick always wanted to run the Foaming Quart and in 1939, three days before the out-break of the war, he took over the pub from Bill Baddeley. Prior to Bill being landlord, the pub was run by Elijah Mayer and his father James before him.

At this time the Quart was only very small, it had a smoke room and a bar, only enough room for about 20 people, and the biggest room on the premises was the kitchen. You see most pubs in those days were what we knew as 'Pinch pubs', the type of old pub in a terraced front room or a couple of cottages knocked through. That's how the pub stayed until I had it changed and modernised to its present layout.

Beer at this time was only 4d a pint and cigarettes 2d for five and whiskey 6d, but in those days a penny was a penny and times were hard. All the beer was on draft and hand pumped through lead pipes which had to be cleaned out with a long wire brush. There can't be many landlords around now who've served beer at 4d a pint pumped through lead pipes!

Also until the 1960s, when I had it piped over, the canal arm came right up into the pub car park, and many a time when the Dray-men were delivering the beer barrels one would roll off the wagon and land straight into the canal feeder.

Another memory I have of the early days was the 'short back and sides' on a Monday morning at the pub, when pensioners would come in for a pint and get a free haircut! Usually a short back and sides.

I started work at Chatterley Whitfield and helped my parents to run the pub between work, helping behind the bar and doing cellar work. I suppose at the time I was learning my trade but never looked at it like that back then.

When war broke out I was exempt from 'call up' having a reserved occupation as a miner so I joined the Home Guard. I first joined the Brown Edge Unit and then later the Norton Unit and became a Corporal there. Our headquarters were at the top of Norton in the Parish Rooms opposite the Vicarage on the crossroads. We would do all our drill there: marching, learning about arms and fighting tactics etc.

When we were on night watch we had to take our uniform to work with us and go on duty straight after work, a very long day as we started at the pit at 4.30 am. Mind you we did get paid for 'night watch'. I think it was 1s 6d a night.

Throughout the night watch we manned a big machine gun and I can remember being on duty with one fellow and a German aircraft flew over and this chap said to me, 'here let me have the gun, I think I can bring him down'. Well, I looked at him and replied, 'dunner be so daft, you wunner do that with this, and if he notices us firing on him they'll be nowt left of Norton!'

It wasn't until after the war that we were shown a stockade of grenades and ammunition that was kept at the side of the parish rooms, I suppose that the officers knew they were there and it would have been handed out if the Germans had invaded. I often think that if a stray bullet had got in there then the whole building and surrounding area would have been flattened!

The air-raid shelters for Norton Green were in the front playground of the school and if the sirens went off most people from the village would use them. I remember one old chap whose name escapes me, he would come rushing out of his house holding a wooden box and he'd always shout 'Is it one of ours or one of theirs?' Presumably the box was full of money or important papers or something.

I put the first dartboard up in the Quart in 1940, when darts was in its infancy and it took off with the locals like wild fire. You see a lot of the younger men of the village came to our pub and the older men seemed to use the White Lion just up on Endon Road. It was around this time that I helped to set up a local league. It was the Smallthorne and District League and we entered our team along with a lot of other pubs from the surrounding area.

In 1948 I took over the running of the pub from my father with my wife Vera and I applied for a full alcohol licence to sell spirits and beer. I had to go to Stafford Assizes to make the application which was a bit daunting but it all went through OK in the end.

By this time we had a very successful darts team and had topped the Hanley and District League in 1948 and 1949 going 75 games without defeat. 1950 was our finest season as we became the Midland Counties Area Champions and reached the finals of The Peoples National Darts Team Championship playing for the Lord Lonsdale Challenge Trophy. The finals were held at the Horticultural Old Hall London on Saturday 10th June 1950. We got to the finals by winning the following fixtures:-

1st round	Brown Edge W.M.C. 'A' Stoke-on-Trent.	2-0
2nd round	Star Hotel. Ironmarket. Newcastle.	2-0
3rd round	Queens Head. 'A' Kidsgrove.	2-0
4th round	Royal Oak. Bignall End.	2-0
5th round	Railway Hotel. 'A' Halmer End	2-1
Section final	Coach and Horses. 'A' Stafford.	2-0

Shropshire, Staffordshire and Derbyshire Divisional Finals:

Semi Final	Vine Inn. Retford. Notts.	2-1
Final	Holly Bush. 'B' Rugby	1-2

Unfortunately we didn't win the competition but had a fantastic weekend away and a memory we can keep forever. The event programme write up on the Foaming Quart team was:

Eight teams, each the champions of its area, are competing tonight for the premier award of the dart's world. Here is a glance behind the scenes into the lives of the stars whose skill has brought these teams national fame.

Alex Hancock (captain) is a busy man, for he is the Landlord of the Foaming Quart, a pub in this tiny village of 600 people, and is also team secretary. As No 1, he sits next to miner Arthur Bowler. Then comes Leslie Hall, a silk dyer, who scored both winning doubles in the area final. James Mountford, No 4, has been a miner for 27 years and is a colleague of James Mellor. Arthur Adams - who scored both game shots in the area semi-final and Bill Wright. In eighth chair sits Sampson Sheldon, at 20 the 'baby' of the team and a coal face worker. Ex miner John. J. Hancock, a brother of skipper Alex is now in corporation employment. Then there is Frank Harrison, who broke a leg after an earlier championship match and hobbled on crutches to receive his area winner's tankard. Miner Joseph Gerrard and John. T Hancock balance the team of twelve.

Cards was also another regular game played in the bar and at one time the lads had a game going for quite a time with about £7 in the kitty, which was a lot of money at that time. Well word must have got around because one day when I was out and about I bumped into Sergeant Randles from Baddeley Green and he collared me and had a quiet word with me: 'What's this I hear about this big game of cards at your pub?' Well after that the lad's moved on to dominoes.

We also had a pub football team full of local lads and we played our home games in one of Reg Simpson's fields up at the Old Hall. I remember the pitch was on a slope so the games always swung each half with the team kicking down bank always having the advantage. There was another team in the village run by John McLaughlin and they played their home games in a field off Ball Lane belonging to Heakley Farm.

There was always lots of laughter in the bar with all the local characters, there was old Bub, his mate Fub, Jim Gerrard, who always had a fag stuck in the corner of his mouth, but the biggest character of them all was Danny Savage. I could write a book on the things Danny got up to; he was always up for anything, for a bet or a bit of fun. One time a bunch of us bet him that he couldn't row down the feeder from the Quart to the Cut arm in a tin bath. Well Danny took up the challenge and the date was set. Word of this challenge soon got around the village and around 50 people had turned up to watch and I think Danny got a bit nervous and sent word that he was unwell so everyone went home disappointed, but there was lots of other good times we had with Danny and everyone liked him.

I carried on running the Quart until 1970 when I handed the pub over to my daughter Maureen and her husband John Flowers.

Being brought up around darts in the pub, Maureen was a natural at the game and she went on to become the England Captain and No 1 in the world and with all her success in the game the Quart became the most famous dart's pub in the world.

The Foaming Quart.

Maureen Flowers, the World's Number One, Women's Darts Champion and England captain.

LEFT: 'Hancocks'. From left, Sam, Jack and John, enjoying a pint in the Quart.

Foaming Quart darts team 1950s.

The Foaming Quart, Norton Green at the turn of the century. At this time the landlord was James Mayer and his wife Minnie. James was known locally as 'Chink'.

BELOW:
Locals at the rear of the White Lion, Leek Road.

Norton Home Guard taken outside the parish rooms on Norton Lane.

Norton Home Guard, Alex Hancock front row, second right.

Foaming Quart darts team 1951. Back L-R, Jack Hancock, Frank Mountford, Frank Pointon, Don Sheldon, Sampson Sheldon, Frank Harrison. Front L-R, Alex Hancock, Jim Mellor, Jack Hancock, Gordon Major, Joe Gerrard.

Foaming Quart darts team 1959/60. Sid Cope,—?—, Gordon Major, Les Hall, Jim Mellor, Alex Hancock, Frank Harrison, Frank Mountford, Sampson Sheldon, Alfie Wright, Arthur Bowler, JT Hancock, Joe Gerrard, Jimmy Mulliner.

Maureen Hancock (Flowers). Second row, from front, third from right. 1950s

Ladies darts team early 1970s. From left, Maureen Flowers, Vera Hancock, Iris Mountford, Lorraine Challinor, Iris Hancock, Barbara Gibbons.

Bertha Hancock (Carp) - Cockshead Well dressings

I grew up at Little Heakley Farm one of seven children, my parents were farmers and they worked hard. There was no well at the farm and my father and the family had to fetch all the water from a tap by Cockshead Cottage.

As well as the farm they had a produce stall in Burslem market. They had to do all the buying in for this. They were very busy so we children made our own entertainment. Our life consisted of home and school and we didn't go very far from either. One of our pastimes was 'licker jumping'. This entailed jumping over the River Trent. We would jump a few 'lickers' then walk along for a while, then jump some more. Sometimes we fell in and got wet, which was alright so long as it wasn't school the next day, because we wore the same clothes the next day, sometimes for the week!

In the summer we used to build dams across the Trent so that we could swim and paddle. The water was so clean then (it wasn't silted up). Another thing I remember, I think I was about nine at the time, we children dressed up as queens. It was all unofficial, just children playing and we concocted it all up ourselves. I was a queen in a hand-me-down dress from one of my sisters and I wore an old curtain for a train. The other children were my brother and sister, Bernard and Beryl, Margaret and Joan Brown, Celia Holmes, Betty Lovatt, Olwyn Lear and Malcolm and Sheila Knott. Their grandfather looked after the canal, it was woe betide you if he caught you riding along the tow path. The crowning took place by the well at Cockshead Villa farm where the Lovatt family lived. I drank a glass of water from the well and someone took a photograph. Our parents got involved and made refreshments for us.

The dressing of wells and springs is unique to Staffordshire and Derbyshire, and the following poem tells of such an event happening at Cockshead. The date and origins of the poem are uncertain but likely to be written by a member of the Fox family. (NGHG)

COCKSHEAD WELL-DRESSING

Now ladies and gentlemen both young folk and old
I think you'll agree with me when my story is told
The story is short that I'm going to tell
Of an old fashioned spot they call 'Cockshead Well'

Now Cockshead you know has a nice country view
With houses surrounding and gardens a few
Where Norton bells with their merry peals ringing
Can be heard all around while the wild birds are singing.

In years gone by there stood an old mill
But now things have altered and all's very still
Except the canal where boats you'll see plenty
Going down loaded and coming back empty.

Now the old mill house is a nice quiet spot
With gardens in front and that's worth a lot
Of beautiful daisies, pansies and stocks
Not very far from old engine locks.

Where Mr John Burton, our late friend you know,
Attended his duty, daily but slow
There's an old saying 'slow and steady wins the race'
Mr Burton was always a man of good pace.

Not very far from the old engine locks
There's another place, old Jackson's boat dock
Where boats were repaired and so neatly done
By late Mr Jackson and William his son.

Now another late friend I think you'll agree
Was William Johnson, a good man was he
Like Mr John Fox our late friend I'm sure
Was a very good man and so kind to the poor.

There's two more neighbours you'll know of them of late
The late Ned Stubbs and William Snape
Who day after day had their work to go through
Work there was plenty but pounds but a few.

Now two more old friends and then I've done
Were late John Bould and Edwin his son
Who when they were living kept reaping and sowing
Took pride in their garden and what they were growing.

I've reason to respect Cockshead House I am sure
Our family have lived there for a century or more
For it's turned over from one to another
Until it's got down to Herbert my brother.

I've never had such a thought in my head
That a well-dressing would be held at Cockshead
It's money that makes the mare go they say
Let's try better next time and never say nay.

Let us thank Mr Walker, a true honest chairman
Of the Council of Norton, for it's a fair one
And the rest of the Council so willing and kind
Such true hearted gentlemen as you'll ever find.

Now Mr George Fox you all know so well
Straight forward and honest, as sound as a bell
To find such a gentleman staunch and so true
I think you'll be busy the wideworld through.

About Harold Fox I'm just going to tell
Will Johnson, A Lovatt, and E Mosedale as well
Who worked very hard for very many hours
Dressing the well with such beautiful flowers.

Now Norton Brass Band played their music so sweet
I think you'll agree that it was a treat
I thought at our Herbert's front door
That I'd never seen such a Cockshead before.

Those people from Cockshead I'm sure they'll think
When they go down to the well for a drink
The work of rebuilding the well they adore
Is a credit to Mr Tom Davis I'm sure.

So thanks to the bandsmen and all who took part
They're always willing to give a good start
At charitable causes and needy cases
They always turn up with a smile on their faces.

There is an old saying I've heard people say
Where there's a will, there's always a way
So keep in remembrance the words I say here
Let's try for another well-dressing next year.

Let's thank Mr Boulton a kind friend is he
Who lent us the ground so willing and free
Our respect for him may we ne're think to sever
But wish him good luck and prosperity forever.

Now Cockshead to me is a nice country place
So now I must close on account of space
All those who are here please try to endeavour
To keep Cockshead Well in remembrance forever.

Five members of my family were at Norton Green School at the same time. The teachers were Mr. Rostance (Head), Mr Downing, Miss Hand, Mrs Shenton, Miss Holland and Miss Walker the infants teacher. I was one of the first to go to the new secondary school at Endon. Prior to this all the pupils started and finished their education at Norton Green School. We used to have PT in the girls playground as there was a wall between the boys and girls playgrounds. People would watch us from the footpath having PT. At Endon as well as the three R's we learned how to iron and fold shirts and wash socks, which we had to take to school with us. We had a celebration when I was at Norton Green School - I think it was the 1937 Coronation year. We all dressed up, I was Britannia, I wore a brass fireman's helmet, and a white dress. I can't remember about the trident.

I don't remember very much about the war except the night a bomb was dropped at Biddulph Moor. We jumped out of bed to see what had happened. We weren't afraid as long as our parents were there we felt safe.

I was married to Eric Hancock soon after the war had finished and things were still on ration. My mother got the coupons for the food for the reception which was held at the chapel. People helped out and contributed if they had any coupons to spare, and a local man did the catering. The actual wedding ceremony was held at Norton church where my father attended. I wore a white dress (which I still have). My mother saved the coupons to buy the material, and it was made by a local dressmaker. We had our honeymoon in Southport, it was November but the place we stayed at was very nice with a good landlady who made us very welcome.

As a child I had music lessons and learned to play the piano. When I was about sixteen a member from the church (Billy Dawson) came to see my parents to see if I could be the pianist for them, as I had played occasionally there. I wasn't consulted as to whether I would like to, but I did as I was told, that was how it was in those days. I have been the chapel organist now for more than 60 years.

Every year Norton Green chapel held an outdoor service on the green. It was called the camp meeting, it was a big event in the village. A hay wagon was brought from Back Fold Farm. I would stand on a chair then climb on to the wagon to play the organ (harmonium) which was loaned by one of the residents. Chairs and forms were arranged on the green and the minister conducted the service from the hay wagon. These camp meetings were also held at other local chapels and people from the village went to them as well.

I remember one Sunday when the parson who was to speak at the service at the chapel didn't turn up, so my husband Eric was persuaded to step in and do it. He was very nervous about this as he wasn't a local preacher. My sister Jessie wrote a poem about the situation. She wrote a lot of poetry about everyday things, some of them quite funny.

WHEN THE PREACHER DID NOT ARRIVE   Jessie Lovatt

The congregation were all there
Having said a little prayer
Bertha playing music from here and there
Still no preacher what shall we do?
Don't worry, don't get in a state
She may turn up although she's late!
Five past six, no she's not coming
Now who is there in the running?
All the preachers are planned out
What is there to talk about?
No I can't do it, couldn't you?
I'm more settled in a pew,
No use, said Eric, I'll fill in
I'll do my best, I'm not so dim
So we sang a hymn or two
Rousing ones and quiet ones too
The notices and collection done
The sermon now it has begun
Eric took for his text

THE LORDS PRAYER
A good sound text
Trouble was with his specs
All steamed up and ringing wet
He could hardly see the print
All blurred up, that thick black ink
But he plodded on most determined
Gave us a right good sermon
Now they want him on the plan
Because he took it like a man
Don't rush him though he's not sure
Although he's done it once before
He will have to do another
It will save a lot of bother
Should the preacher not turn up
He will have his notes
Right there beside him
Should he need them
They will guide him.

Cockshead well dressings.

Cockshead Well Queen, Bertha Hancock in centre.

LEFT: Camp meeting at
Norton Green 1943.
From the left Billy Dawson,
Sam Unwin, Rev. Roberts,
Bertha Hancock-Carp on
the piano.

BELOW:
Sunday School Camp
meeting August 1941 on the
Village Green.

Camp meeting 1940s on the Village Green.

A sermon from the hay cart. This hay cart was borrowed from
Mr Barber of Backfold Farm.

Bertha Hancock-Carp as 'Britannia'.
May 12th 1937 fancy dress for the
coronation of King George VI.

Foundry Square Camp meeting.

Village Green Camp Meeting c1945. Bertha and Jessie Carp on left with matching coats. Others include:
Maureen Newman, Annie White, Annie Heath, Roy Dawson and Pauline Mayer.

Anonymous - Childhood memories

I was a child of the early 1930s and lived in the terrace below the Methodist Chapel, then called Leek Road. At that time there were six working farms in the village, five shops, a coal merchant, the school, now a residential home, two public houses, the White Lion now a dwelling and the Foaming Quart. There were few detached houses apart from the farms, mostly terraces, Leek Road, Foundry Square, Bews Buildings and Trent Terrace. The last two became flooded during severe weather conditions.

All the farms had working horses, except Mr Boulton at Yew Tree Farm who had the only tractor in the village, we children called him 'Aeroplane Joe' on the quiet. I had to collect milk from the farm in an enamelled milk can and with practice I managed to swing it full circle without spillage. Mr Barber, Back Fold Farm, delivered milk from a horse-drawn float. The council houses were built where Mr Sherratt farmed and Mr Arthur Boulton's farm was in Foundry Square opposite the school. He once came to the school to demonstrate the use of a flail. There is now a newly built house on the site which was Mr Worthington's Yew Tree Farm. The hairdresser's business next door was a sweet shop, where pennies and halfpennies were spent.

There were seasons for games in the playground. Hop Scotch, skipping ropes, ball games, top and whip. On Empire day the Union Flag was raised by the head teacher as all the children gathered around the flag pole for the annual event. One summers day all the school children had an outing to Heakley Hall Farm and had a wonderful time playing among the sand hills - no longer there. The river at Gorsey was blocked by older children to make a pool for swimming.

The long summer holidays from school were spent playing in the hayfields and paddling in the brook, taking along a jam butty and a bottle of water, then home at tea time hoping the geese at Cantrell's farm would not chase us along the footpath.

Lower Flatts Farm was worked by the Cantrell family and they raised pigs. All windows and doors were closed down the row during the day when pig swill was boiled. 'Phew'. Mr Cantrell never approved of the allotments which were worked on his land during the war.

Very few vehicles were on the road at this time, Brown's buses on the Burslem to Leek run and Turner's, Brown Edge to Hanley. A regular car was a blue Buick driven by Dr Devenport on his daily round. Nurse Clay the midwife did her round on foot. Most days a train could be heard puffing along the railway track across the fields beyond Norton Green.

We had a blind neighbour who lived in our row and I sometimes asked him the time as he passed by, I was fascinated by his special pocket watch with Braille figures.

The Co-op bread van did a daily delivery and Bill Taylor's hardware van did a weekly service. A man wearing a turban seemed to appear once a year, selling at the door from a big suitcase. I kept out of his way.

Road repairs were interesting to watch especially when the huge steamroller came along. It gave us a bit of a fright. A Saturday night social at the chapel was the highlight of the week, mostly games, musical chairs, spinning the plate etc. The chapel anniversary was the time of the year for a new frock and shoes and many hours of singing practice with Mrs Mayer, ready for the special services.

The wireless provided many interesting programmes and entertainment, Just William, Children's Hour, The Ovaltinies, Dick Barton Special Agent etc. A favourite was Saturday Night Theatre, which began with 'this is your storyteller, the man in black' and hopefully the battery or accumulator would not give up. Workers Playtime was a lunchtime programme during the war.

There were no road lights at all in the village, so a flash light was a must if out after dark. I was once taken to Bews buildings to look at a fox which had been shot in the fields, I felt very sorry for it. The next time I saw it, it was being worn as a fashionable fox fur - the in thing during the 1930s.

I became a pupil at the village school during 1939, with the building of the air raid shelters, the issue of gas masks and the sound of the air raid sirens - and evacuees.

A sketch of Heakley Hall Farm around 1930.

A view of Leek Road (now Endon Road) around the turn of the century.

Backfold Farm.

Mr Sutton with his terriers outside the farm cottages at Backfold Farm.

Turner's buses, There was a saying in the village that you could set your watch by Sammy Turner.

Members of the Sutton family who lived in the farm cottages at Backfold Farm.

Clifford Boulton - Foundry Farm

My mother's parents were coal merchants named Rogers and they lived and traded at the cottage next to the school. Father's parents farmed Lark Hall in Bagnall before moving to Foundry Farm in Norton Green.

When my grandfather came here the farmhouse was in the Foundry House. It belonged to Lord Norton. Then he made the two double fronted back to back houses, 141 Leek Road and 21 Foundry Square into the Foundry Farm House. My grandparents moved into the larger house and the Mottram family into Foundry House.

Foundry Farm was the site of the iron foundry. Mr Rostance the headmaster of Norton Green School researched it and he used to come and talk to Father about it. Father dug up a great lump of iron ore from the farmyard one day which had been left from the Foundry.

When my father married, grandfather and grandmother Boulton moved to the Adams Croft at Ball Green and my parents Arthur and Hannah continued to farm at Norton Green and it was here that my sister and I were born. I spent the first 10 years of my working life on the farm working for my father. Both the farm and the land were rented from Lord Norton and it was spread out over various sites around the village, about 60 acres.

I went to Norton Green school and then to Endon when I was eleven, leaving at fourteen to work for my father. There was no choice in the matter, you did as you were told in those days. Father had injured his leg when he was about nine and they took out his knee cap and he had to wear a leg iron. He could do anything on the farm - he could even build the hay stacks. The only thing he couldn't do was bend that leg.

We used to get up at about 7am and milk 18-20 cows by hand before breakfast. I would set off on foot to deliver the milk in two cans, with a half pint and a pint measure. The customers would bring their milk jugs to the door and I would measure the milk out to whatever they required. I used to go up the main road, down Woodland Avenue and across the Duke Bank Terrace, this took most of the morning's milk. Some was sold at the farmhouse door and the rest was fed to the pigs. The evening milk was collected by Nestles from Congleton, they collected the milk from all the farms round here. During the war, when everything was on ration, every Christmas we had a big box of chocolates off them tied up with a ribbon and delivered to the door; we used to look forward to this.

We sold milk, eggs and poultry at the farm door which was always open to customers, but when the war was on we had to shut up at 9pm because of the blackout. The milk was always fresh and some people had it delivered twice a day. When I got back from delivering the milk I used to say 'by the time I get to middle age my arms will be so long, my wrists will be dragging on the floor!'

My father was a hard taskmaster, if he saw you reading a book he would say 'put that down! I've got a job outside for you.' He would say 'take the scythe and cut the thistles in those two pasture fields this afternoon, it's a nice day.' I could use the scythe OK but next morning I'd a job to get out of bed! Father would say 'you're not finished yet, the way to cure it is the old fashioned way - that, that brings it on, will take it off' and sure enough it did.

We had two working horses, Bob and Betty and I loved them. A friend of mine, John Walker who married my sister Margaret used to come to the farm when he was a lad, and we used to take the horses down over the draw bridge to the pasture along by the canal - we had the ground along as far as Bullers. We'd get on the horses and say *'I'll race you'* and off we'd go.

I worked on the farm for ten years and although I enjoyed it Father didn't pay very much. There were about ten of us lads in Norton Green who used to go out together at the weekend. I could only go out once a week then I'd spent up, so I decided to leave farming and go to work at Bellerton Pit. My first weeks wage was £6-6s-6d and I felt like a millionaire! Mother and father said I must be mad to leave farming but for the first time in my life I could start saving and have some money in my pocket.

Fathers dairy herd out in the pasture.

Hayricks in the farmyard. Father was renowned in the parish for the building of the best hayricks even though he had an injured leg.

Bob, one of father's horses - in those days we had no tractor and the horses did all the work.

Clifford Boulton in front of Foundry Farm.

My first car purchased after leaving employment at the farm and working at Bellerton Pit.

Bob and Betty the farm's working horses.

A view from the front of the farm looking out onto Endon Road.

LOT 15.

Coloured Blue on Sale Plan.

THE CAPITAL

FREEHOLD SMALLHOLDING

known as

Foundry Farm, Norton Green

comprising

**A brick and tiled House and Farm Buildings at Norton Green
with Pasture and Arable Land**

Bounded by the Caldon Canal.

Area, 18a. 3r. 39p. or thereabouts.

THE **HOUSE,** with the Farm Buildings and Garden form an island site with frontages to Leek Road, Foundry Square and Ball Lane. It contains Lobby, Sitting Room, Kitchen with range and cupboards, Dairy, back Kitchen with sink and copper, Milk Room with copper, Cellar and four Bedrooms, and has a large Garden with Pigsty and e.c.

Main water is laid on. Electricity is available.

THE **FARM BUILDINGS** comprise brick and tiled Stable for 2, tying for 13 cows, part with Loft over, and Barn.

Let to Mr. Arthur Boulton on an annual Ladyday tenancy at a rent of **£40.4s. 0d. per annum.**

A disused Boat Dock adjoining the Canal is included with this Lot.

SCHEDULE.

O.S. Map No.	Description.						Area. Acres.
Parish of Norton-in-the-Moors.							
409	Pasture	...	...	...	...	...	2·961
Pt. 411	Pasture	...	...	...	...	...	8·129
447	Arable	...	...	...	...	...	3·401
Pt. 448	Arable	...	...	...	...	...	3·364
449	Foredrift	...	...	...	...	...	·225
Pt. 479	House, Building and Garden	...	...	...			·535
City of Stoke-on-Trent.							
Pt. 2920	Pasture	...	...	...	...	...	·077
Parish of Norton-in-the-Moors.							
Pts. 406 & 411	Boat Dock	...	...	...	...	...	·305
							18·997 or 18a. 3r. 39p.

Tithe redemption annuity, 17s. 2d.

NOTE. *This Lot is sold subject to an easement in favour of Leek Rural District Council in respect of a water pipe crossing O.S. Nos. 411 and 2920, and their right to extend this pipe across O.S. No. 409; also to the right of the occupiers of Cockshead Cottages to take water from the well in O.S. No. 411.*

This Lot is also sold subject to and with the benefit of all existing rights of way and in particular subject to a right of way for all purposes in favour of the owner and occupiers of Lot 17 in this Sale between the points marked A and C on the Sale Plan.

This Lot is also sold subject to a wayleave in favour of the N.W. Midlands Joint Electricity Authority in respect of 1 stay.

An extract from the sale of Lord Norton's Estate 1947, lot 15 Foundry Farm, Norton Green.

Doris Fox (Mellor) - Foundry Square

I was born in 1919 at number 18 Foundry Square. I was the youngest of eight children the oldest being Henry who was sixteen when I was born. Our house had two rooms up and two down plus a kitchen. The toilet which was at the top of the garden was emptied once a week. There were no dustbins in those days, all the ashes from the fires in the row and the toilet contents were taken away by horse and cart at night by the 'night soil men'.

At the top of Foundry Square was a shop where you could buy all your groceries. You could take a jar and buy syrup. Butter, lard and cheese were also loose and had to be weighed up. They also sold paraffin which was stored on the other side of the entry.

There was a family in Foundry Square with six children, I won't tell you their name but there were three daughters and three sons. Two of the daughters used to go to Manchester on the train and they came back with all sorts of things which they had stolen. I remember my sister buying a fox fur off them. Eventually they got caught at it and I'm not sure but I think they may have gone to prison because we didn't see them for a while!

One of the neighbours was Lucy Haywood. She and her husband lived in the front room of her parents' house. Every year, she seemed to have a baby, quite often twins who never survived. They were so poor, they weren't fed properly and the Vicar of Norton Church had to bury them. He used to say 'whatever is happening to all these children that they are dying all the time?' When twins were born, I used to go to see them and my mother would say 'they won't be there long' and it was true.

Foundry Square used to be called the Yellow Row. It got this name because the people who lived there at one time had yellow skin because they worked at the Foundry which was behind the row of houses. Opposite the Yellow Row was Foundry Farm where my granny and grandad Mellor lived before they went to live at 127 Endon Road (now 168), which was once a pub called the Horn Inn. They had two cows and my brother Dave and I used to go round Norton Green delivering the milk from them. They also had a horse and cart which they used for fetching corn for the cows, pigs and poultry. I can remember collecting leaves from the trees which grew by the side of the meadow where Clifford Avenue is now. We put the leaves in a 'braddish' bag and they were used as bedding for the livestock.

The house which is now 40 Foundry Square used to be a shop. Some people called Edwards came from London to keep it for a while. Mrs Edward's sister, Hettie King, used to come and stay with them occasionally. She was a famous male impersonator and we children used to sit on the wall while she marched up and down with a cane singing 'I'm Burlington Bertie'. Then we would follow behind singing as well. We really enjoyed it and it was a real treat as she always gave us all a few sweets. We always looked forward to her coming again.

Next to Edward's shop was a row of six cottages which have now been knocked down. In one of these cottages lived a Mrs Banner who used to make herb beer in a galvanised bath. She would sell it and she always said 'I'll bae the bottle back' as you were walking off.

My aunt Alice, my father's sister, who I never knew, lived at Keepers Cottage at the top of Ball Lane; she tragically died before I was born. She'd been shopping at Baddeley Green and was on her way home along the canal path which was frozen over. Some how, she fell in, probably crossing the drawbridge at Long Butts and went under the ice. All her shopping was scattered on the ice and it was my father who helped to get her body out. She's buried in Brown Edge churchyard right by the steps with two of her children who died in infancy.

My sister Ruth left school at fourteen and went to work in service at the Heakley - Heakley Hall Farm. Although it was very close to where we lived she used to live in. Mr and Mrs Ball and Mr Ball's brother Enoch who we called 'Nocky' lived there. Nocky, I remember, had a hammock in the trees. He used to go to fetch grains from Parkers Brewery in Burslem with a horse and cart. The cart was steaming when it came back through Norton Green. I can still remember that smell now.

I used to go and stay with my sister at the Heakley on Saturday nights when Mr and Mrs Ball went out socialising and came in late. I remember they grew sweet peas in the garden and I used to go and pick them. They paid me one and sixpence for this and they gave the bunches away to their friends. I also collected eggs; I loved going round there after school.

Outside the door at the Heakley was a big stone slab with some sort of religious signs on it. It fascinated me. As I remember, you went down some steps and there was a door leading somewhere, to a tunnel I thought, but it was very dark and I didn't go through.

There was a sand hole in the field next to the Heakley and I would go and watch the sand martins building their nests. I can't remember any sand being taken out of there; it must have been before my time.

There used to be five stone cottages called Sheldon's Row on the main road opposite the Old and New Halls. One of the people who lived there was Polly Holdcroft, who was known locally as 'Barm Polly'. She used to sell sugar, paraffin, matches and tea at the back of the house. Every week she went to Burslem to fetch cakes in a basket and then went round Norton Green selling them. I can remember my mother would buy them off her. Polly also used to get balm from Parkers Brewery in Burslem and sell that to people who wanted to make herb beer. My mother made this and we had to go collecting nettles, yarrow and buckbean.

Danny and Esther Savage lived at Bews Cottages, behind the hairdressers on Endon Road. They were a lovely couple and they had one daughter Hetty. Danny was a night watchman. In his spare time he used to make pegs and sell them and I've still got some of them now. I don't know if Danny had been in the Navy or not but on one entire wall of his house was a painting of a sailing ship. It used to fascinate me. I don't know what happened to the painting when the house was knocked down because it was on the actual wall. Hetty married a Dawson and they went to live in one of the Cockshead Cottages, down by the canal. Old Esther was a lovely lady; she would always give you a hug when you went in.

We always called the Old Hall the Akhust. This is because, before my time, the story was that someone was killed with an axe in one of the rooms there. I had a friend who lived there for a while and she showed me which room it was - and it was always kept locked.

In the fields behind the Hall there was a tree, I think a lime, there was a fork in it and sap used to collect in a hollow. The miners, whose eyes were troubled by the dust from the pit used to bathe their eyes in it, but I don't think the tree's there any more.

The former caretaker's cottage next to the school, 183 Endon Road, was a coal yard when I was a girl. They always delivered with a horse and cart. The house that is now 179 Endon Road belonged to a Mrs Sheldon and in the front room of the house she sold all kinds of animal foods in wooden coffers. You could also buy potatoes and Mrs Sheldon also sold ice cream. I used to go as a girl and turn the handle of the churn which was made out of wood and had paddles. I had to pack the ice around the churn. I don't know where the ice came from but it was always in a braddish bag. Mr and Mrs Sheldon also sold coal from their yard in Yardley

Street where the bungalow is now.

In the house next door was a Mrs Hudson. We used to call her 'Polly Hatter' because she sold hats from her front room. There was a bay window at the time to display the hats. There mustn't have been enough money in selling hats because she started selling fruit and veg.

The house that was 'Up the Vale' paper shop was once the farmhouse to the land where the estate was built. I think it was called Hall Farm. Sherratts kept the farm, mother and son, Charlie. My sister in law Liza used to go and clean for Mrs Sherratt. After Mrs Sherratt died the council bought the land and built the estate.

The house which is now 161 Endon Road was a pub called the White Lion. Glen Goodwin kept it. He had three daughters and Amelia was the oldest then May, Flossie and one son Charlie. I think he went working at the Co-op. Women were not allowed in the pub and nobody under 21 either. The men played cards and dominoes there, but I remember it used to shut early about 10pm. In the house next to the chapel lived a Mr and Mrs Machin, a very well spoken couple. Mr Machin was blind and every night when the pub opened he used to walk down to the White Lion for a drink, tapping the path with his stick as he went along. My mother used to do their washing and I would take it up for her. It was a big basketful and I had a job to carry it up the bank. They paid my mother half a crown and Mr Machin always gave me the exact money although he couldn't see.

The Waste (what we call the Tank Field now) which is on the right hand bank of the Trent is where the gypsies came once a year. They came in the traditional covered vans pulled by horses which they tethered by the side of the brook. They stayed about three days and they sold saucepans and milk cans and the tins the miners took their snappin in, also tin bottles. I remember at night, they would light flares which they stuck in the ground around their camp. I think these were made from old cloth soaked in oil because I can remember the black smoke coming off them. There was never any trouble with these gypsies. They just used to knock on the door for fresh water. When they left they always went Brown Edge way although I don't remember whether they stopped there.

We children played on the Waste. We made a game using bolts which we got from Taylors the hardware shop at Norton which was where the betting shop is now. We used to stand them up in the dirt and throw metal washers at them to knock them down. We also had metal hoops which we bowled along with a metal hook. We went all round the village and even up to Norton. We played hopscotch, marbles and skipping and we made stilts out of old tin cans and rope. Something else we did which was really very dangerous was to jump onto the step at the back of the bus, I think it was Browns, hang on and get a free ride up to Norton. Of course it wouldn't be going very fast in those days.

I can remember the older men coming from Brown Edge and Norton and perhaps Baddeley Green, to sit in a hollow at the top of the track which goes down to Heakley Hall Farm. They played cards and gambled there and if they caught us spying on them they would chase us off. It was illegal to gamble at that time. The men would also gather on a Saturday morning having a chat and waiting for the 'bookie's runner' to collect the bets at the stumps at the beginning of Yardley Street. In those days it was known as the 'Iron't' because it was down this track that the iron ore was taken to the Foundry from the mine near Lower Flatts Farm.

When I started school in 1924 Eva Proctor was the infant school teacher at Norton Green School. Other teachers were Miss Hand, Mrs Shenton, Miss Bailey, and Mr Rostance was the headmaster. He lived on Crate Bank, and later he had a bungalow built on Ball Lane below Upper Heakley Farm. A Mrs Powditch came to work at the school while I was there, and I used to take bets to Mr Beardmore's for her. The Beardmore's were a lovely couple, they had three children Mary, Nellie, and Edith. Edith died in the fever hospital in Tinsters Wood, Brown Edge.

I was at Norton Green School until I was fourteen. Everyone was, except those who passed out to go to high school. I started work at Bullers, Milton, luckily I got the job before I left school, so I went straight from school to work. My job was to smooth off the insulators after they had been fired. Then they were dipped and fired again. We worked 6-6 which was a long day.

I then got a job at Wades in Burslem; the hours were not so long only 8-5. I could get a bus there, 5 pence (5d) return, but my ticket lasted two days because I used to walk home. Sometimes I went on my bike and that didn't cost anything.

Like so many of the men from Norton Green, Doris's father Tom fought in the conflict of the Great War 1914-1918. He joined the North Staffordshire Regiment and fought in Northern France only to be injured early in the campaign. Having recovered at the Beaufort War Hospital in Bristol he was soon back into the theatre of war in France. In March 1918 Tom was taken prisoner whilst fighting at Bullecourt and spent the remaining months of the war in captivity. On Tom's return home to Norton Green he received a personal letter from George V thanking him for his part in the war and wishing him happiness now he was among his family again. (NGHG - www.norton-green.com for more on Tom's war experiences)

Mary Ann, Edith, Ruth, Doris (babe in arms), Joe, David - Mellor.

Henry and Doris Mellor taken outside
18 Foundry Square.

Joseph and Mary Mellor of 141 Leek Road,
later to become Foundry Farm.

Miss Hetty King the famous music hall entertainer, a frequent visitor to the village.

Tom Mellor, back row, third left, with the North Staffordshire Regiment.

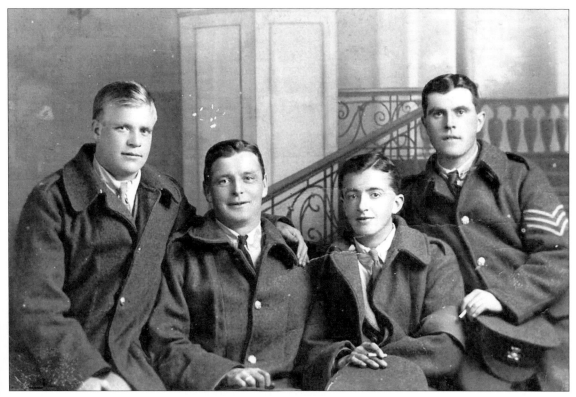

Tom Mellor, first left, with army pals.

Tom Mellor, middle row, second left, North Staffordshire Regiment.

A day trip out for the returning servicemen of the parish in 1918.

Selina Mellor.

RIGHT: Mr and Mrs Ball
of Healey Hall Farm.

**The delivery van of Mr Ball of
Healey Hall Farm**

Henry, Tom, Mary Ann, Edith and Ruth Mellor.

BELOW:
Tom Mellor's welcoming home letter from
Buckingham Palace 1918.

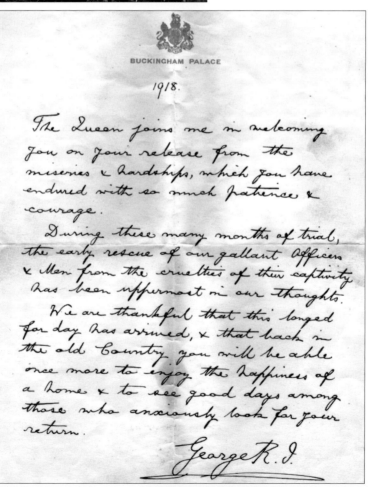

BUCKINGHAM PALACE

1918.

The Queen joins me in welcoming you on your release from the miseries & hardships, which you have endured with so much patience & courage.

During these many months of trial, the early rescue of our gallant Officers & Men from the cruelties of their captivity has been uppermost in our thoughts.

We are thankful that this longed for day has arrived, & that back in the old Country you will be able once more to enjoy the happiness of a home & to see good days among those who anxiously look for your return.

George R. I.

Coronation Celebrations 1937

May 12th 1937

The coronation of George VI was a celebration the whole village was involved in. A coronation committee was set up by members of the school with plans for celebrations that matched anything anywhere in the country. Funds were raised by donations from local businesses and surrounding gentry, also a collection from house to house with even the poorest of residents giving generously.

Coronation mugs were bought from Midwinter's Pottery of Burslem to give to the children for a keepsake. Fireworks were purchased along with flags and ice cream. Invitations were printed; and balloons, medals for the children's sports, instruments for the local band were all hired. There was tea, sugar, toffees, sweets and an array of food bought for the 'tea' at the Methodist Chapel school room for the elderly and for the children of the village at the school.

A competition for the best dressed house was held with a cash prize for the winner, and the children were invited to attend in fancy dress. Processions through the village were to be led by the village jazz band, with the party going on into the early hours of the morning.

The total cost of the celebrations came to £21-0-05. We can only imagine the joy that was had on this day. It seems the hard work was mostly down to a few special people like Mr Wilfred Rostance who was Headmaster at the school and the backbone of many activities in the village.

PROGRAMME OF EVENTS

1.30 pm - Assemble children in the schoolyard around the flag.
   Children singing:
> God save the King.
> Here's a health unto his majesty.
> Land of my fathers.
> Dear little shamrock.
> Land of hope and glory.
> Rule Britannia.
> '3 cheers for the King and Queen.'

2.00 pm- Procession formed.
   To include: Village jazz band.
> School children in costume.
> Parish Councillors.
> School managers.
> Ex service men.

2.30 pm - Service in the Methodists Church conducted by Rev Cook.
After the service the children to march down to the school for the judging of the fancy-dress.

4.00 pm - Coronation tea.
   In the council school for the children.
> In the Methodists schoolroom for the old folks, widows and blind persons.

5.00 pm - Each child given a dish of ice-cream.

6.00 pm - Sports on the field.

9.00 pm - Dance in the council school.

10.00 pm - Fireworks.

12.00 midnight - Conclusion of events.
   To include: National Anthem.
> Auld Lang Syne.
> 'Cheers for the King '

A personal account of the celebrations for the Coronation sums up the nation's mood and that in our village. Mr Wilfred Rostance wrote the following in the minute book of the Coronation Committee of Norton Green:

When coronation day was over, I fell to musing over the events which led up to it.

Two years ago on May the 6th 1935, we celebrated the silver jubilee of the late King George V and Queen Mary, but a few months later on January 20th 1936, he passed away, and on January 28th he was laid to rest in St George's Windsor amid sorrowing mourning of his subjects.

King Edward VIII was proclaimed King and his coronation fixed for May 12th 1937. But on December 11th 1936, he abdicated in favour of his brother, who was proclaimed King George VI.

King Edward VIII's action caused much consternation. He wished to marry a twice divorced American lady, Mrs Wallace Simpson.

This was against the will of the people and the government under the fearless leadership of Mr Stanley Baldwin our prime minister who faced the serious situation in a calm manner. He refused to discuss a morganatic marriage and as Edward refused to renounce his desire to marry below his rank a deadlock ensued and in the end he abdicated. Baldwin has been referred to as England's greatest statesman since Cromwell.

During these hectic days, England was perfectly calm, and work and business went on as usual. The radio proved its worth in this crisis, and after Edward had signed his abdication, he broadcast a farewell to the nation giving his reasons for his actions.

So George was proclaimed and so that arrangements would not be upset, he proclaimed 12th May 1937 for his coronation.

And so the empire settled down to the business of preparing for the coronation of King George VI. The events of the month of December had unsettled the nation and much as Edward had been loved and respected by the people, some were wondering if loyalty to the crown was to be maintained. George had a wife, a real true born lady of Scotch descent and already she was loved by the people, and to further strengthen their love, she had two little daughters Elizabeth and Margaret Rose, who were the nation's favourites.

So the newly proclaimed King George VI and his consort Queen Elizabeth gradually established themselves at the head of this Great British Empire.

The nations of empire swore their loyalty to the crown and as months passed they were firmly established, and Edward as Duke of Windsor was only a memory.

All talk was of the coronation, and as the merry month of May arrived so did royalty and notabilities of all nations coming to England. Every part of the empire sent representatives and the great city of London, the heart of the empire, was gay with decorations and people of every clime and tongue. Truly there was enthusiasm for the greatest crowning the world had ever seen.

Radio, television and the press did their work splendidly and the event will be ever remembered because of the permanent recordings and films which have been made.

So on May 12th 1937 King George and Queen Elizabeth were crowned in Westminster Abbey, amid pomp and splendor by the Archbishop of Canterbury, before 1000 people. Thousands perhaps millions lined the streets and cheered the royal pair on their return from the Abbey.

Thus was the crown firmly established, and England carries on - as only the English can carry on. The will of the people was done and democracy rules.

And what happened in our village?

Like all places in the empire arrangements had been made and everyone was anxiously awaiting 'the day'. Jubilee was remembered and so were two coronations, but what of this?

The weather was not too favourable, but what did it matter? Houses were gaily decorated and every one was happy.

At 1.30 pm the children and people assembled in the school playground and how heartily those patriotic songs, how they cheered and what a sight as 220 flags were waved aloft. The true British spirit.

Then the procession through the village. The village jazz band in their patriotic costumes, the children in fancy dress.

Service in the Methodists church. How we turn to our church in times of rejoicing. We thank our God for all that kingship means.

Teas for children and old folk. A sea of happy faces. Words cannot express it.

Sports for all in the field.

Darkness falls, dancing in the school. And so on until close.

The King.

Old Lang-Syne

And then home.

What memories we carry of a day which will live forever in our hearts and minds. The King crowned; the throne stands supreme. The British Empire is firmly welded. Britain is on the pedestal once again for all the world to admire - dare I say fear? I dare because the might of our empire is the true solution to world peace.

And now that King George VI is crowned we can say with true meaning!

'God save the King.'

'Long may he reign.'

W. Rostance. June 1937.

Patriotic Songs

At NORTON GREEN the festivities were in no way behind those of other wards of the Parish of Norton-in-the-Moors. With Mr. G. W. Walker as Chairman, Mr. W. Rostance, Secretary and Mr. Henry Proctor, Entertainment Secretary, the enthusiastic Celebration Committee had ensured a successful day's rejoicings. For the children a great day had been prepared, and at the Norton Green Schools their rendering of patriotic songs was a great feature. Mr. J. Jack addressed the children. A gay procession was formed and in the Methodist Church a service was held.

On the sports field a delightfully varied programme was carried out. Tea was provided for the children in the Council Schools, and in the Methodist Schoolrooms the old people were entertained. Coronation souvenir mugs for the children and gifts for the old people were distributed. A display of fireworks, followed by a dance in the Council Schools, ended the proceedings.

An extract from the Staffordshire Evening Sentinel reporting on the festivities at Norton Green. Courtesy of Staffordshire Sentinel Newspapers.

King George VI
Coronation Celebrations at Norton Green

THE CORONATION COMMITTEE

respectfully request the pleasure of

at a

CORONATION TEA

to be held at

THE METHODIST SCHOOLROOM,
NORTON GREEN,

ON WEDNESDAY, MAY 12th, 1937,

at 4.30 p.m.

Please bring a Knife and Fork with you.

The invitation that was sent to residents to join in the celebrations at the Zion Methodist Schoolroom. Note the bottom

Old Folks and Widows and Blind Persons.

to whom invitations were sent.

Ridgway

Mr & Mrs. Lowe.
Mr & Mrs. J. Lowe.
Mr & Mrs Bailey
Mrs. Abel Holdcroft.
Mrs. Joe Bailey.
Mr & Mrs. Jarvis.
Mrs. Grimes.
Mr Baddeley Senr
Mr. Heath Senr
Mrs. Grimes.
Mrs. Robins.

Mr & Mrs J. Cope.   Mr & Mrs. A Pointon.
Mrs. Holdcroft.   Mr & Mrs. Rowland.
Mrs. Sherratt.   Mr. C. Mayer.
Mr & Mrs Scragg.   Mr & Mrs. J Boulton.
Miss Hodgkinson.   Mr & Mrs. Ford.
Mr. C. Brocklehurst.   Mr. J. Rodgers.
Mrs. Johnson.   Mrs. S. Sheldon.
Mrs. Clarkson.   Mr & Mrs. Junt.
Mr. J. Costance.
Mr. Barnett.

Norton Green

Mrs. Griffiths   Mrs. Whitwell
Mr. Robinson   Mrs. Glover.
Mr & Mrs. Buckley.   Mrs. Dean.
Mr. J. Dale.   Mrs. Pointon Senr
Mr. J. Foster.   Mrs. Pointon Junior.
Mrs. Brownsett.   Mr. Sutton
Miss Massey.   Mr & Mrs. J. Sheldon.
Mr & Mrs Lawton.   Mr. J. Cook.
Mr & Mrs. Worthy.   Miss Docksey.
Mrs. W. Sargeant   Mr & Mrs. J. Mayer.
Mrs. Ellis.   Mr. & Mrs. S. Bailey
Mr & Mrs. Felton.   Mrs. W Sheldon.
Mr & Mrs. Capewell.   Mr & Mrs. J. Clowes.
Mr. C. Clowes.   Mrs. A. Holdcroft.
Mrs. Goodwin.   Mr & Mrs. S. Worthy.
Mr. J. Machin.   Mr & Mrs. C Banner.
Mr. J. Holdcroft.   Mr & Mrs. A. Steele.
Mrs. S. Holdcroft.   Miss Mather.
Mr & Mrs. Pegg.   Mrs. Stubbs.
Mr. G W. Walker.   Mr. & Mrs. Johnson.
Mr & Mrs Bradley.   Mrs. W. Heath.
Mr & Mrs Armstrong.   Mrs. Gaskell.
Mrs. Knight.   Miss Mountford.

An extract from the Coronation minute book showing the list of all residents invited to the chapel tea.
Old Folks and Widows and Blind persons.

Darren Gerrard - Memories of Yew Tree Farm

When I was asked to write this I thought I was too young to add anything of value or interest. But on reflection I suppose I have seen as many changes to our village as most, because when I was growing up in Norton Green it was a thriving community with Trentside School at the heart of village life. Along with the school we had a butcher's, a chip shop, post office, paper shop, garage and petrol station and four corner shops. Reg Simpson who would deliver fruit and veg by horse and cart and the fish man who would visit on a Friday. Davenports Beer did home deliveries. Now the village is a very different place, all of the above businesses have long gone, so here are some of my memories of when I was growing up in the village.

I was brought up at Yew Tree Farm on Endon Road during the 1970s and 80s. The house was demolished in 2000, but was replaced with a new house and buildings, still retaining the same name. The house was once part of a threshing barn and had been converted to a dwelling in the 1800s I believe. We think of a barn conversion as a modern concept but obviously not.

All the rooms in the house had very low doors and ceilings with exposed oak beams that were jointed with wooden pegs, as were all the massive beams in the adjoining barn. I could reach up and touch all the ceilings in the house without stretching. There was also a couple of brick barns, haystack, outbuildings and two pig-sties in the rear yard.

At one time, many years ago, owners of Yew Tree Farm such as the Reptons held quite a considerable amount of land and property in the village and surrounding area, but it seems that most of it was sold off at various times probably due to inheritance taxes. One of the owners was a Benjamin Yardley who had six properties built at the entrance to the farm around the 1870s, which is where the name Yardley Street comes from.

When my family moved in we only rented the house, buildings and large yards to the front and rear. We had no central heating just an open fire in the living room to heat the entire house. I can remember many a winters' morning waking up and scraping the ice off the inside of the tiny windows, then rushing downstairs to have a warm by the roaring fire. The fire was always lit when we got up, the first thing to be done every morning by either my mum or dad, we never used a drawing tin - the old Sentinel paper from the night before was just the right size.

I lived there with my elder brother, two younger sisters, my mother Pauline, originally from Burslem, and father Samuel, whose family have lived in Norton Green for over 130 years. It wasn't until recently after carrying out some family research that I found out that my father Samuel was named after his father Samuel, who was named after his father Samuel. Prior to this my forefathers were millers in the Waterhouses and Ellastone areas of Staffordshire until Samuel Gerrard moved to Norton Green around 1870 to work as a miner.

I don't recall too much about my grandad other than going down to visit him and grandma when they lived in a flat on Trentside Road and playing dominoes with him. He was housebound, his health not too good, and I was young, so I never had the opportunity to have long chats. My brother on the other hand was lucky enough to be taken out many times by grandad on his walks to collect herbs from the fields around Heakley Farm for herb beer, and through the fields around Woodhouse Lane, collecting watercress from the streams and blackberries from the hedgerows, then off home, for tea, where grandma would lay on one of her 'spreads' of fresh sandwiches, beetroot, pickles, trifle and an array of homemade cakes, tarts and egg custards - all baked in the oven range.

Now my grandma's cooking I can remember, she always seemed to be cooking, it was the first thing that hit you as you walked through the door, it made you instantly hungry, what a fantastic cook she was. I can remember at Christmas time she seemed to be swamped by a sea of mince pies that she had cooked for members of the family, all stacked up in tins ready to be collected. I suppose that having a growing family through the 2nd World War you had to be able to provide good home cooked food for them. Grandma certainly did that.

My uncle told me that when they lived up Ball Lane grandad had three vegetable plots which he attended to after doing a full day's work, and these provided most of the ingredients for his family's meals. His two sons were both given a shovel or fork and told to help, there was no choice on the matter either.

Before moving to Ball Lane they lived at Yardley Street and grandad had a village allotment along with his brother James; they were where Selworthy Road is now. Even when times got better and the family moved to Trentside Road on the newly built council estate, grandad still grew all his own vegetables.

My aunt says that during the War when food was rationed and the word got around the village that some tinned salmon was due in at a local shop, grandma would send the children to the shop to take it in turns to queue up, swapping places with other brothers and sisters at meal times so as not to lose their place. This tin of salmon would have to go a long way and would be an eagerly awaited meal. I suppose both my grandparents' passions of gardening and cooking were born out of necessity and became a way of life.

My father to say the least was a bit of a character and was very well known around the village. One New Years Eve they held a fancy dress competition down the Quart and my dad went as Worzel Gummidge and I think he won second prize. But the ironic thing was that the landlord's daughter won first prize and wore a trilby hat, boiler-suit, wellies and a tray of eggs - and she went as my dad.

Living at Yew Tree as a child was a happy experience as there was always something new to see and do. You see my father worked as a builder but still kept plenty of animals at home as well, as he had worked on a farm when he left school until his national service call up, so I think he always had a passion for farming and the simple life of self-sufficiency. We kept at various times hens, pigs, cows, turkeys, pheasants, ducks, geese, goats, sheep, along with all other manner of domestic pets and we still had room for a considerable vegetable plot.

At one time my dad brought a donkey home called Joey, and I can remember him giving it a drink of brown ale from a bottle that the donkey seemed to enjoy very much. Now this donkey always seemed to be breaking out of the pens and going off to visit female donkeys in the area - we had to fetch it back from as far as Tongue Lane. Once we were camping out in the yard with friends when we heard this almighty crash followed by the sound of hooves around the tent. The next thing the tent came crashing down around us, the donkey had pulled all the guide ropes and pegs out running around the yard. We tried for a while to catch him but failed and ended up going to fetch my dad out of the Quart to get him in.

Not long after my mum was in the post office when Cyril Mottram asked her *'Pauline, do you know who practices the blasted trumpet down your way at about 5 o'clock in the morning?'* To which my mum replied 'that's no trumpet, that's Joey our donkey!'

We never seemed to get too attached to any of the animals as they came and went quite frequently. Once we had a couple of young pigs, I think they were large whites, and on one occasion when we had friends around, my dad decided to let them out of the sties and one of the pigs took a liking to Stephanie Ziemann and began to chase her around the yard! I can still vividly picture Stephanie shouting 'Mr Gerrard do something' while everyone looked on with great amusement.

Later my dad decided to sell one of these pigs to George Cantrell who lived just down the track at Lower Flatts Farm. When George turned up to collect the pig he was wheeling a large muck barrow which we thought very odd at the time, anyway after he paid my dad he promptly picked the pig up plopped it in the barrow and took some bailing string from his pocket and tied it on. Then off he went down the track wheeling the barrow as normal as anything with the pig squealing blue murder! Later we found out that instead of having a ring put in the pig's nose to stop it rooting up the soil, as was the practice, George had used an old bed spring!

My brother and I along with other friends used to go and help George milk his cows, he had a small herd of Jerseys. After we'd finished milking George always asked us into the house and would show us all different types of weapons that he and his father had collected over the years. There were cavalry swords, sabres, muskets and even a blunderbuss. In the kitchen he kept hens under some of the chairs with a bit of straw for bedding and mesh around the legs to keep them in. Whenever he needed an egg he'd just reach in and get one.

George used to drive an old van with a pair of antlers fastened to the front grill. My father bought these antlers from the farm sale when George packed in farming and moved to Leek.

When I started school at Trentside, Mrs Lloyd was the Headmistress then; she was very well liked by everyone, pupils and parents alike. You started in Mrs Bedson and Mrs Dean's class followed by Miss Holly, Mrs Taylor, Mrs Lancaster, Mrs Coclough, Mrs Gratton, Mrs Courlette then Mr Bagnall in that order. I was never really much of a scholar and always felt locked in. I spent a lot of time looking out of the window. But I suppose looking back it wasn't too bad.

I remember when we went from the infants to the junior classes we used to go to Burslem Drill Hall every Friday morning for PE because there were no facilities at the school. We went to the baths at either Burslem or Tunstall for swimming lessons. I enjoyed sports at school and in 1979 we won the area cricket cup; the final was played at Norton Cricket club against Ball Green. I always played in goal at football but we weren't that successful. I suppose you could say that football was in my blood as my father and grandfather both played football for various teams, including ones in the village.

My dad always told us that when he was young, the lads from the village never had a proper football to play with but used to get a pig's bladder from the butchers and played with it on the 'Green' until it burst.

At this time we had a village football team, started by Mr Bednall who lived in the village. We played on Sunday mornings in the Burslem Lads and Dads league under the name of Norton Green Rangers. I think we wore yellow strips. Later we had a junior and senior team and when we were in the seniors it was run by a friend's mother Esther Dawson. Even today it would be a little odd for a woman to run a lads football team so you can imagine what it was like for her back in the late 1970s, early 80s! I think at the time we didn't give Esther the respect and credit that she duly deserved and I often think that she was incredibly brave to take on and run the team, with a bunch of teenage lads.

But every first Sunday of the month I used to go missing from the team as most of the lads from the village went trapping for John Travis at Brown Edge Shooting Grounds. We got £3.50 for a morning's work which was more than you got for a week's paper round. This didn't go down to well with Esther and she would sometimes suspend me, but being the kind soul she was she would soon forgive me and I'd be back playing next week.

In other spare time we spent a lot of time down the brook fishing, at this time it seemed a lot cleaner and alive with all kinds of fish and wildlife. We used to catch sticklebacks, bullheads or as we called them bullnogers, stone loach, brown trout and minnows. There were also plenty of crayfish and freshwater oysters that littered the river bed and each spring the brook would come alive with elvers (baby eels) that would swarm together in masses as they made there way down stream - we would call these young eels 'seenees', I don't know why but everyone new them by this name.

We would always see plenty of water voles as well, their holes were in the sides of the brook, but I haven't seen one down there for many years now and I don't think there are half the different types of fish there were twenty odd years ago.

1977 was the Queen's Silver Jubilee and we had a party at school to celebrate the occasion. Everyone was given a coronation mug and I think we had a special holiday as well.

All around the village different streets were making preparations for their own street parties so my mum and a few other parents from neighbouring houses got together to arrange their own party. They decided to hold it at our house because of the large garden at the front. Well us kids from the area had the job of cleaning out our barn to use in case it rained. After a couple of days cleaning we had to whitewash the walls to brighten the whole place up.

On the day of the party we had a fantastic time. All the parents brought food, drink, cakes and trifles. It was all laid out on tables on the lawn and we hung flags and bunting around the house and garden. After everyone had eaten we children joined in all kinds of games and races. Then later in the afternoon it began to rain and we all took all the chairs and tables into the newly whitewashed barn to continue with the party.

Another occasion when mums and dads would get together to help out at events was Bonfire Night. Families around our area would build one at the end of Yardley Street on a patch of waste land. Building the bonfire was a job for us kids, and me, my brother and friends from neighbouring houses used to start collecting firewood months before and stack it in our barns and hayshed. But on the night of the fire, the job of lighting the fireworks and fire was down to one of the dads who would make sure everything was done safely.

Later in the night when the fire had died down most of the parents would bring chairs out of their houses and sit around the fire chatting into the night. It was really community minded in those days - not that long ago to be honest.

I wouldn't say I really believe in ghosts but living at Yew Tree all members of our family had some strange experiences to say the least. My youngest sister when she was very young occasionally talked about a silver lady, and we never knew if she had seen something or it was just her imagination. One morning when my other sister was sitting by the fire watching television she swears she saw a black cat walk across the room and disappear into the fireplace.

We all heard things creaking in the night and on a number of times my father, who would dismiss things of this nature as 'pure rubbish', would get up after hearing what he thought was one of us children going downstairs; but after going downstairs there was nobody there!

Probably the most frightening of experiences was had by my brother who was lying in bed one night when he felt something grab him by the ankles and pin him to the bed! He says he was that frightened that he couldn't even scream or shout out for help. This happened when he was around twenty years old so you can't just dismiss it as childhood imagination.

In 1987 I married and moved just around the corner into Yardley Street and slowly all us children left home one by one. Then sadly and most suddenly my father passed away in 1990 and my mother only stopped at Yew Tree Farm for another couple of years before moving to Hanley to be nearer my sisters.

My father's funeral was led by a horse-drawn hearse, which was quite a spectacle at the time. I remember that the church at Smallthorne was absolutely packed and after the service we all followed the procession on foot to Burslem Cemetery where he was buried.

Now I have a daughter of my own and I hope that she will have some fond memories of living in Norton Green herself.

Grandma and Grandad, Samuel and Sarah Ann Gerrard.

My father Samuel Gerrard
and myself, 1967.

Norton Green allotments, now Selworthy Road.

A view of Ball Lane prior to any properties being built.

Ball Lane Victory Party 1945. Members of my family included in the photo are Marjorie, Ida, Joseph and Irene Gerrard.

Norton Green allotment holders summer 1936. Grandad - Samuel Gerrard back row second left.

Norton Green football team c1910. Grandad Samuel Gerrard, middle row, second left.

My father Samuel Gerrard's funeral procession, 1990, heading to Burslem cemetery from Smallthorne. (Courtesy Staffordshire Sentinel)

Trentside cricket team, 'local school champions'. From left: Richard Bryan, Peter Dawson, Jonathon Corbishley, Mark Flowers, Darren Gerrard, Adrian Barker, Gary Davies, Alan Richards, Wayne Flowers, Mark Goodwin, John Wallace. (Courtesy Leek Post and Times)

Norton Green Rangers Football team 1978. From left back row: Steven Ward, Alan Dawson, Mark Walton, Darren Gerrard, Craig Sutton, Oliver Slinn, John Wallace. Front row, from left, Andrew Gibbons, Wayne Flowers, Peter Dawson, Mark Flowers, Philip Bednall, Andrew Walton, Neil Ferriday.

David Smith - My Father was a Leek Man, my Mother a Norton Greener

My parents Stan and Alma moved to Pointon Grove in the 1950s when the council estate was built. Pointon Grove was originally called Cherry Grove and was the first street to be completed; my mum and dad were one of the first families to move into these properties, moving from Endon.

I think they moved to Norton Green to be nearer my mum's family (Sheldon) who had lived in the village and surrounding area for generations. The oldest relatives I know of living at Norton Green, were my Great Grandparents Sampson and Hannah Sheldon of Foundry Square.

My mother Alma Doreen Sheldon was born in Foundry Square, the daughter of Doris and Arthur. My Grandfather Arthur served in the army during the Great War, 1914-1918 and continued his service until 1920. Sadly he died at the age of only 40 leaving my Granny to bring up the family. Luckily enough she had many relatives and friends in the village to support her.

My mother attended Norton Green School, some of her class mates were Bertha Hancock, Winifred Pickford, Mabel Sutton and Mary Frost. Leaving school at 14, I think she began work at the mills in Leek, presumably she met my Dad, Stan who was a 'Leek man' while working there.

My Dad, James Stanley Smith was born in Leek in 1922; he told me that when he left school he joined the Army at the age of only 15, giving a false date of birth. I know that during his service he travelled abroad because occasionally he would quote us a few words of Arabic, so I imagine he served in Egypt.

When he met my Mum and they married he was working as a miner in Stoke-on-Trent and while working at Sneyd Pit he lost his left leg, just below the knee.

Dad enjoyed all country pursuits (like poaching!) and losing his leg didn't stop him. I can remember him telling me of when he was out poaching rabbits with his friend and they ran into trouble with the police who chased them, They were making their getaway when they ran into some heavy mud, and Dad got bogged down and had to unbuckle his false leg and leave it there. Luckily the Police didn't catch them or find his false leg stuck in the mud and dad managed to retrieve it later the same night - and return home with a catch.

We always had dogs at home, always a whippet or two, and these dogs earned their keep as they went everywhere with dad, catching rabbits and hares. Ferrets were always kept in hutches in the backyard and were also used to catch rabbits. Dad made his own purse nets - he would sit for hours making these long nets in the living room and people came from all around to buy them. He taught us kids to make them and it became second nature to us. I'm sure I could still make one today. I suppose some today would think rabbiting a cruel sport, but in those days it helped to feed your family.

Mum was always busy cooking and looking after us kids and any neighbours or relatives who called around would be invited to stay for dinner or tea. Family meant everything to Mum and she always put it first, even before herself. I still live at my family home and have very fond memories of our house when we were all here; plenty of visitors which gave the house plenty of life and laughter.

'Grandad' Arthur Sheldon (born 1895)
taken in 1920.

LEFT:
Sampson (born 1869) and
Hannah Sheldon with family
taken at the rear of No. 54
Foundry Square.

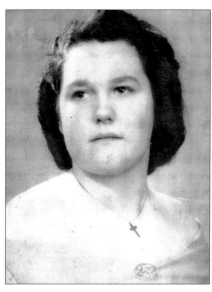

'Dad' James
Stanley Smith,
aged 16,
during his
service in
Egypt.

'Mum' Alma Doreen Sheldon (born 1925).

Foundry Square Victory celebrations
1945. Great Granny Sheldon seated
front left with friends and family.

Dad and friend with
one of his many
working dogs.

Gertrude Joan Pickford - Bugs Gutter

I live on Endon Road now and moved here from Bews Cottages where I was born in 1924.

Sadly Bews Cottages are no longer, they were just behind Endon Road (formerly Leek Road) close to the River Trent. They were also locally known as 'Bugs Gutter'.

I lived there with my grandfather, father John Henry, mother Dora - everyone knew her as 'Dolly' - two brothers, John Henry and Kenneth George and three sisters, Winifred Jane, Irene and Clarice May, I also had another brother, David, who died at only two weeks old.

My mum and dad met at the Ideal Skating Rink in Hanley. My mother was a Sherratt and was born at Rock Cottages, Brown Edge. She talked really broad, I suppose you would call it slang now; we never spoke like that but could fully understand what she was talking about.

My father was a policeman and in his spare time he used to conduct the village band, they played bazookas - you can make the same sound with a comb and some tissue paper. Mr Rostance the school headmaster approached my dad to ask him to run the band. They wore a blue and yellow outfit and were called the Jazz Band. They'd play at local events in the village, also at carnivals and fetes at Norton and Brown Edge. They won many prizes locally and managed to raise a lot of money for charity.

I was in the band along with a couple of my aunties and friends including Nelly Beardmore. One of the songs we sang along to was 'Blaze Away' and it went like this:

> Make a bonfire of our troubles,
> Watch them blaze away,
> Watch them go up in smoke clouds,
> Never to return another day.

My grandad played the cornet in Brown Edge Brass Band, and every Sunday morning he would play hymns at home and my mother would sing along. I can see her now singing 'When the rolls call up yonder, Jesus shall reign.'

Grandad's favourite meal was as he called it 'ringers and tinbonnet' - its proper name was 'hangers and tinbonnet', bacon and cheese cooked on the open fire. My mother would never cook it because the cheese would sometimes have maggots in it back then and you could see them on the plate when the cheese was melted, it would always turn our stomachs but it never bothered grandad.

There were three cottages in Bews Cottages and we lived on one end. The middle cottage was occupied by the Hancocks. All the Hancocks were known as 'Cud' - I don't know why but everyone knew them as that. Jack Hancock used to cobble shoes on the hearth in the living room; Mrs Hancock was a dressmaker and used to run a 'fund' for a charity shop in Burslem. Dick Hancock would dress up as a woman and act the fool at local carnivals and collect money for charities.

The Hancocks kept ferrets for rabbiting and one day one of the ferrets got loose and no one could find it. Well the next morning my grandad, who was working at Chatterley Whitfield pit at the time, began to put his clogs on when out jumped the missing ferret!

When we grew older we used to go to dances at Ball Green Club and to the 'Tuppeny Rush' at Smallthorne 'Scratch'. We never told father where we went though, I think he thought we were at Chapel. Well if a chap had walked us home, I'm afraid sometimes he'd be in for a severe shock! You see Mr Hancock would be waiting at the bottom of our entry with his shotgun! He didn't give them any chance to hang around, he'd see the lad off and tell us to 'get in and get straight to bed' and we did.

Dan Savage and his wife lived in the other cottage with Dan's mother who always wore an apron made of a potato sack, even on a Sunday. We called this type of apron 'Brannish' Dan was a real character, he was a short stocky man who wore old fashioned thin rimmed round glasses. He always reminded me of Popeye but if my mother heard us calling him that she'd tick us off.

Dan used to mend clogs and he'd put metal studs in them, we could always hear him coming down our entry, it's a wonder he didn't dig the road up with them. He also grew a lot of comfrey and other herbs and would make something up for anyone who was ill. He'd say 'here have a dose of this, you'll soon be up 'n' about'.

Dan would do anything for a bet and once he climbed the highest chimney at Chatterley Whitfield Pit because someone had dared him. People would use the chimney to forecast the weather; they'd say if the smoke went straight up it was going to be fine and if it went one way it would be wet and the other way meant it's going to get windy.

They were a real authentic family and when the landlords - Bews of Burslem - decided to have electricity installed they didn't want it put in because they were afraid of it. We were the first in the row to have it installed and I couldn't stop switching it on and off, I was so amazed, everywhere was so bright with all the lamps.

My Aunty and Uncle Sherratt also lived in the village, at Sheldons Row, another row of cottages that is no longer there, which overlooked what they now call the Tank Field but we always called Balley's Field because Ball's from Heakley Farm used the field in those days.

I remember going coal picking with my Uncle Ken down by the canal, there was loads of it lying around there at this time; people even used to go swimming in the canal and would dive down and bring up lumps of coal

Others who lived in Sheldon's Row were 'Old Bub' as we called him and he would walk around the village singing hymns, but never did anybody any harm though. 'Old Polly' also lived there, and she would walk to Holdcroft's in Burslem two or three times a week and buy two big baskets of cakes, walk home and sell them around the village.

My sister Winnie at one time lived at the 'Old Hall' with her husband Roy and daughter Christine. It's a very old place with lots of history and they reckon that Lord Norton once lived there. There was a passage from the front door with a room leading off it that had been sealed off; if you knocked on the wall it would echo. Our Roy was tempted many a time to knock it through but never did. There was one room that had a big open fire in, but no matter how long the fire was lit the room always seemed to be freezing. There was a stain on the ceiling of the living room that people reckoned was a blood stain - every time it was painted over, it still kept coming through!

Christine was learning to play the piano so our Winnie decided to take a photo of her playing the piano in one of the rooms, only when the photo came out it had all faces on it! Christine never wanted to go upstairs on her own and would tell her mum and dad 'that wulstation's there again' - she meant Alsatian. Even after Roy and Winnie reassured her, Christine was adamant that the dog was still upstairs with her! They began to wonder if she was psychic. Later they moved from the Hall and went to live at Brown Edge.

We also moved - to one of the terraced cottages fronting Leek Road just in front of Bews

Cottages. We all knew our neighbours in those days, on one side of us was Fred Dawson. At one time Fred took out two bricks from our adjoining wall where we had a wireless on a stand. No one knew about the hole except Fred, until one Sunday evening when we began to hear shuffling noises coming from behind the wireless, so father moved the wireless to find out what was happening and found the hole. Well he went round to see Fred, 'What do you think you're playing at?' and Fred replied 'I wanted to listen to Sunday Night Half Hour!'

Other neighbours were Turners and Dawsons; the Turners were nicknamed 'Tushers' and Ezra Dawson we knew as 'Whiskers'. There was also the Beardmore's. Mr Beardmore, my friend Nellie's dad, used to take bets for locals, which was illegal back then. I can remember my father would wrap a sixpence up in a note he had scribbled and ask me to take it to Mr Beardmore. Everyone was really friendly back then, if you were playing out one of the neighbours would always ask you 'do you want anything to eat duck?'

Next to Backfold Farm there was also a row of cottages that are no longer there; the families I can remember were: Beamers, Booths, Haywards, Holdcrofts, Lancasters, Harrisons, Gerrards, Baddeleys, Broughs, and Banners. There were also two very small cottages in the farmyard of Backfold Farm, I think there was only about four steps before you got upstairs, and I can remember that Mabel Sutton lived there with her family.

At this time we all had outside toilets and they would be emptied by the 'Night Soil Man' - we knew him as the 'Muck Man'. He would come around emptying the toilets at night and you could set your clock by him. He had two buckets and would spill the contents everywhere, up the entry, up the road and over his clothes; goodness knows what a state they were in! If you had your windows open when he was around you'd know about it too! He'd shout, 'Breath it in, it'll do your coughs and colds good.' Oh the smell it was awful!

The 'Rag and Bone Man' also used to call around the village and if you had something for him he'd give you a balloon or halfpenny. The only thing was that he seemed to talk very strange to us and we could never understand what he said, so we just smiled at him.

There were lots of shops in the village also at this time. Where the Village Bakery is now used to be a chip shop twice, then an ironmonger, then a butchers twice, belonging to Bratt's then Travis's, before it became the bakery.

Going up the bank towards Norton there was an ironmongers, grocers and chip shop that later became the Post Office. Just after Yew Tree House there was also a pub called the White Lion, which also became a chip shop later.

My Mother used to tell us that there was also a bonnet shop in the village that sold hats and shiny patent shoes, and where Grace's Hairdressers is today was once a very small school where you had to pay one penny to attend. Lots of children couldn't afford to go though because a penny was lot of money in those days. I remember when it was a toffee shop run by Mrs Haydon and we used to buy chocolates and sweets there.

The Foaming Quart pub was run by a family called Baddeley as far back as I remember, then Alex Hancock's father took it over, I think they moved here from Tunstall. Alex later took over the running of the pub after his parents, as did his daughter Maureen and her husband John after him.

There were also plenty of farms in the village, Cantrell's, Corbishley's, Boulton's, Barber's and Sherratt's. Sherratt's Farm was where the 'Up the Vale' paper shop was. The farm was run by Mrs Sherratt and her son Charlie. We knew the farm as 'Charlie Chuck -Chuck's' and you could buy fresh eggs and homemade butter there. My sister made a visit to the farm one day, she told me that she had skipped into the kitchen singing (the doors were always open in those days and you just walked straight in) and the old lady was standing there patting her butter on the kitchen table. She said 'I want Charlie Chuck -Chuck' and the old lady replied 'what do you want him for?' 'Me mother wants some eggs and butter'. 'OK' says the old woman, 'I'll go and get him for you.'

Oh the butter did taste so beautiful and the eggs too, everything was free ranged, everything seemed to taste so much better back then.

I went to school at Norton Green Board School and started at the age of three. I remember on my first day at school, there were about eight of us starting, we were all put in Miss Walker's class. We all sat on little wooden chairs and were all waving to one and another, because it was all new to us. The classrooms were very basic and all the desks had sunken inkwells in them. Mr Rostance was the Headmaster and the other teachers were Mr Downing (who was very strict and once made me do 100 lines before I could go home), Miss Walker, Miss Hand and Mrs Shenton.

We would start at nine in the morning and finish at three in the afternoon. Along with the standard lessons of Maths and English we'd have History, which I enjoyed. We also took cooking and learned how to make sponges and pastries. I can remember making rock cakes too, and we could always take whatever we made home at the end of the day.

Sewing was another lesson I really enjoyed which helped me in my later years as I became a dressmaker and used to make all my own clothes.

We had sports days too at school and would have races like egg and spoon. We played rounders in the school yard. The School was also used for a lot of village events, through the war they held dances there to keep the people's morale up.

One time I can remember that Prince Edward, before he became King (George VI), drove through Norton Green on his way to a private function, and we all lined the road and waved flags as the procession of cars came through the village. Later we held a celebration in the school yard. I can also remember the Queen's Grandfather, King George (V) passing through the village.

There was also the Jubilee of the Queen Mother (Mary) celebrated at the school and we were all given mugs to commemorate the event, I still have mine in my china cabinet.

Through the school holidays we didn't have that much to do so we had to make our own entertainment. In summer we would play in the brook by the bridge - the water was a lot cleaner in those days, nothing thrown in the water. My father and grandad used to catch trout in it. Another place was up at the' Ringle', heading for Woodhouse; my mother would give us a bottle of water and some jam sandwiches and she wouldn't see us until teatime. We would also try to swim in the 'Gorsey' but it was never deep enough - the 'Gorsey' was a little further on than the 'Ringle'.

We used to attend the Chapel up the bank on Endon Road, I can always remember the Harvest Festival. We'd all wear white dresses and walk into the Chapel singing 'Bringing in the Sheaves'. We'd walk in through the front entrance, go down one side, then the other and then onto the altar and lay the sheathes down.

Charity Sunday was also another event we really enjoyed. We would all dress up in our best clothes with white ankle socks and white patent shoes, and then walk around the village with the teachers from school singing outside people's houses as we went on our route. In the evening we would go to the Chapel and sing on stage. When it was all over and we got home we would have to take off our best clothes straightaway in case we marked them.

We didn't go on trips or anything - we did most things in the village. As we grew older we found other things to do. My uncle once sent us a gramophone and on Sunday afternoons we would take it to Balley's Field and meet up with friends. We'd all bring records that we liked and sit around talking and listening to the music, the records though were very fragile so we had to be very careful with them.

When Norton Wakes finished it would come down to the Tank Field and set up there for a while. They would set up a May Pole, play football and all sorts of games. I believe it was in my mother's days that Lord Norton gave the Tank Field to the people of Norton Green.

At 14 I left school and was soon called up to help with the war effort, working at the munitions factory at Swynnerton. I had a good job there as an inspector of Naval Ordnance. My job was to inspect bullets and they would come through the machine like anything. There were no chairs in the workshops so we had to sit on bombs and torpedoes at break time, at first I was scared stiff but you soon got used to it.

The rules there were very strict and you couldn't have any contraband or wear jewellery, watches, earrings, rings or makeup on the factory floor. There were 'searchers' who came around the factory checking if we had got anything on us that we shouldn't have. We were quite lucky though because the men on the factory would often warn us that a search was to begin. I once was caught with lipstick on me and had it confiscated and never got it back.

After working at Swynnerton I worked as a dressmaker in the mills in Leek. I worked at Stannards, Wardle & Davenports and Masons. We worked a 48 hour week over 5¹/2 days, starting at 7 in the morning until 6 at night and worked until dinner on a Saturday. A week's wage was about 10 shilling. But there was plenty of employment and you worked where the money was. If your boss upset you or you got a better offer you could tell them where to go and walk straight into another job.

**A view of Norton Green bridge
around 1940.**

Sheldons Row. These houses were knocked down to make way for Selworthy Road.

Gertrude Joan Pickford by the Village Green.

Gertrude Joan Pickford with village queen.

A local band passing through the village.

Local children playing in 'the Ringle'.

The Prince of Wales (later to abdicate as King
Edward VIII) taken as he passed through the parish
on his way to a private function at Biddulph.
(Courtesy Old Nortonian Society)

Dan Savage with one of his many paintings. Dan was a colourful character around the village and an accomplished artist who reputedly painted the mural on the side of The Plough public house at Endon.

The mural on the side of The Plough at Endon.

Chatterly Whitfield Colliery.
Daniel Savage climbed the large chimney for a bet.

Grace Bosson (Chadwick) - The corner shop, Frobisher Street

My mother and father, Lily and Jim Chadwick, took over the shop on the corner of Frobisher Street in 1937 and lived there for 52 years. My mother's uncle, Jess Jolley, kept it before them at the same time as running the Foaming Quart. When my sister Jean left school at sixteen she went to work in the shop to help my mother who was in poor health at the time.

My father was working at Whitfield Colliery and went off on the colliery bus at 4 am each morning. My mother would also get up and fill the shelves to open at 7 am. One morning she heard the latch go on the door. She asked who it was and a man's voice said 'let me in Misses and I'll tell you what I want.'. She shouted upstairs pretending there was someone in. 'Joe, there's somebody knocking at the door and Jim's gone to work; will you come and see what they want?'. Then she ran upstairs and looked through the window but there was no one in sight. Well it had frightened her so that for a few mornings my dad and Joe Baldwin and Ernie Swindells decided to wait and see if he came again. Well, old Mrs Sheldon down the road was putting up the snappin when her light bulb went, so she put Joe's pit boots on to go to the shop in the dark, so anyone would think she was a man, because she was frightened. My dad and Mr Swindells jumped on her. She said, 'Eh lad, I only want a light bulb!'

During the war food was rationed but if any was left over my mother had a list of customers and in rotation she would let them have extra sugar, butter, and cheese and always at the right price, never black market. I suppose they would have been summonsed if they'd found out. Butterworths, the wholesalers used to ring up. 'Jim, I've got a load of jam here if you've got the money come and fetch it' and he used to go and fetch it.

One day he was on the way back with some cases of jam in the back of the car covered up with a blanket when he broke down on Burslem crossroads and a policeman pushed the car over to safety. He said to dad 'are you flitting?' Dad said, 'Ah, just bits and pieces'. He was so tempted to give this policeman a jar of jam but he thought better of it.

One night Lord Haw Haw came on the radio and said they had hit 'White Field' but he meant Whitfield Colliery. Sirens were going pretty often at that time. One night in the shop there was Mrs Congey Mayer, Lizzie Hancock, Bette Mayer, Sally Sutton, Mrs Sheldon and Mrs Barber - it was just like a gossip shop. The siren sounded and Mrs Congey Mayer said 'Oh if I'm going to die I'll have to go to my old man'. But Sally Sutton says 'Oh, Mrs Congey Mayer, dunner goo, Hitler'll have thee' and pushed her - into the potato hopper. She went into the hopper backwards, legs in the air showing her old fashioned knickers that came down to her knees and the shop was in an uproar. Jeff and my Dad had to pull her out. It was really funny. You see Mrs Sutton was frightened of her getting bombed. I was only very little at the time but I can remember it like it was yesterday. They had such fun in those days. The walls used to be shaking with laughter.

Dad started making the ice cream in the Second World War when things were on ration and you couldn't really get stuff to make it out of. The ministry said it was to be made from dried milk and dried eggs. Well my father said if he couldn't give his kids fresh he wasn't selling it to anybody else's, so he made it from fresh milk and fresh eggs. Len Unwin used to bring a churn of milk late at night and leave it in the yard of the shop and Uncle Jeff supplied the eggs and that was how he made it.

Now one day the ice cream machine broke down and some of the ice cream was lost but he was able to save some and this was the day that the ministry came to test it. It was found to be deficient of fat content. He was fined £5 but they never found out he was making it out of fresh milk and eggs, so he carried on and he used to supply every one with ice cream, Endon Well Dressing, Milton Gala, Brown Edge Carnival - he even supplied the hospital, he even made diabetic ice cream, he just left out the sugar.

I remember the first bonfire night after the war - of course we couldn't have one during the war years. The bonfire was on the waste and at 10pm they were knocking on the shop door saying 'we want ice cream, we want ice cream'. Well my mother and father were churning this ice cream and the queue was down to Foundry Square. It was so exciting because we hadn't had any parties for so long. It was really good fun. . He didn't just make ice cream, he had a bash at making candyfloss. It wasn't a great success because the candyfloss was either huge or not very much at all and he gave more away than he sold.

When I left school I didn't really know what I wanted to do and I moved from job to job never seeming to settle. My father kept saying, "well is this your life? Is this your ambition?' I always used to cut my mother's hair and my auntie's and one day Lizzie Heath asked me if I would do her a home perm and it turned out smashing. Then Mrs Walker said could I do one for her the same. My father said 'would you like to go in for hairdressing?' and I said 'yes I think I would'. Next thing he had enrolled me at the Irving Salon that taught at night. It was opposite the Theatre Royal in Hanley and it was there that I started to learn the trade.

I started to do a bit of hairdressing in my mother's shop and when Sheldon's were selling the sweet shop in Endon Road my father bought it for me. I opened the hairdressers in 1958 and the business thrived. My sister Anne went to work for Kath Fox at Smallthorne but we became so busy that she came to join me as I couldn't manage on my own.

There wasn't much social life at the time, so one year we decided to go out with the customers for a dinner and we went to Sandbach Old Hall in cars, about 20 or 30 of us. Well the next year we decided to go to the Lake Hotel at Rudyard; we hired a bus from Turners, about 68 of us this time, all women. The next year the men were feeling left out and they wanted to come too and the number of people coming to the dinnerings snowballed. The most we took were three bus loads. They carried on for years and now we go to the Foaming Quart just before Christmas and Edna cooks a meal for us.

One year we had a trip down the pit. Kath Jones was the coal queen and she organised a visit down Bellerton Colliery. We went down with the noon shift; they showed us round - we saw men we knew from the village working away. It was something different and we really enjoyed it.

As well as the dinnerings we used to organise holidays abroad. These holidays started before I got married and the first one was to Majorca - sixty women went. We ran a holiday club at the shop and that is how we saved the money. Again it wasn't long before the men wanted to come as well. The most we took was two bus loads to Malta. I used to go to the Co-op Travel in Burslem and book the holidays. When we first went to Spain, Franco was still in power so we had to curb it a bit because there was a curfew after 9 pm. We would have a few drinks and end up as daft as bats because we didn't usually drink! It was so funny!

Every Monday morning I used to go to the Little Sisters Home in Cobridge to do the residents hair. Phylis Hancock would come and shampoo for me and we had about eighteen ladies waiting for us. They were happy to see us and they loved to talk to us. Sometimes my niece Anna Marie came with us. She was only small at the time and she used to go and fetch things for them. They loved to see her.

They were always short of money at the home. It was an old building and needed a lot of maintenance. To raise some money for them we organised a trip for the shop customers to the home. The nuns showed us round and they put on a buffet for us and we paid so much each. Phylis and I got very involved with the residents and they said they would like to see where we lived. I asked Sister Patricia if they could come out one afternoon and we would put on a tea for them. They came out in a minibus and Sister Patricia brought some in a car and we had a lovely time.

At that time there was a couple called Lorraine and Pat who lived at the back of us. Pat was having a nap in the back garden of their bungalow. He woke up to see Sister Patricia looking over the hedge at him. He said to me later, 'Grace, if you ever have those nuns again, will you let me know. I had the fright of my life! I woke up and saw that nun and thought I'd died. Then I felt in my pocket and my money was there so I thought there's no way they would bury me with my money'.

Eventually, the Little Sisters Home closed but we kept in touch with Sister Patricia for a long time. Before the home closed the Mother Superior showed me a large leather-bound ledger with the names of the fund raisers who had donated money to the home and our name was entered into this book. The book was sent to the Vatican and is now kept in the archives and she said our names would never be forgotten.

Irene Gerrard, Grace and Anne Chadwick and Mavis Heath.

Jim Chadwick's Rover
outside his shop at
Frobisher Street
(Formerly Mayer Street).

The corner shop
Frobisher Street
(formerly Mayer Street).

Pamela Bossey,
Grace and Anne
Chadwick with
Hancock's shop in
the background,
Foundry Square.

Lily and Jim Chadwick.

Grace Bosson and Sister Patricia with a resident from the Little Sisters' Home.

Jean Chadwick serving in the shop.

A visit to Bellerton colliery 1965. Elsie Evans, Cath Hancock, Lilian Conliffe, Anne Chadwick, Grace Chadwick, Gladys ?, Cath Jones (the coal queen), and her sister ?, Mr Baddeley. (Courtesy Leek Post & Times)

Dinnerings. Back L to R: Margaret Mullock, Nelly James, Agnes James, Pat Storey, Elaine Richards, Amy Barber. Middle: ?. Front: Sally Turner, Mrs Barratt, Anne Martin, Grace Bosson, Margery Meredith, Jean Nettel.

Harry Lovatt - Cockshead Villa Farm

I was born here at Cockshead Villa Farm in 1919. My Grandfather Snape first came here and rented the property for 2 shillings a week and began market gardening, growing bedding plants etc. There are two hawthorn bushes in the yard overlooking the canal, one that blossoms white and the other red; my grandfather brought them as saplings in his pockets when he moved in. Long before the farm was once a pub called the Cockshead, and it was me who removed the stillage from the cellar that they used to keep the barrels on.

Where the farm buildings are now there was once a mill and they say that it was the first mill to grind flint under water to keep the dust down, but all I know was that there was a large hole of about thirty foot where the water wheel was - and I was the one who filled it in. The mill was fed with water all the way from Knypersley and my mother said she could remember the mill race still running when she was young. When we dig the garden over we always unearth bits of flint - it must be what was left over after the grinding had finished.

We had no running water in the house when I was a lad and we fetched our drinking water from a well in the field; our water for washing we got from the canal that was a lot cleaner in them days. I wish I had a pound for every bucket full I'd fetched back then, I'd be a rich man now! Occasionally fishermen on the cut would ask my mother to make a pot of tea for them and they always remarked that it tasted wonderful from the well.

In 1932 a school teacher from Norton, Mrs Ford, visited us to see if we would vote for her in the up coming council elections, so we asked if she could get us running water. Well nothing ever came of that but shortly afterwards they came from the Council and tested the water from the well and told us it was unfit to drink and we couldn't use it anymore. From then on we had to fetch drinking water in two buckets from Limekiln Cottages until we got piped water in 1946. We had no electricity either until 1950 and I had to pay £5 a pole to have it fed from Limekiln Cottages, which was the nearest property with electricity.

Farm workers from Heakley Hall Farm working in the valley.

Living by the Caldon canal we saw lots of traffic up and down the cut and they used to queue up to use Engine Lock. Most of the barges were pulled by horse or some had a couple of mules. They transported corn, tar, coal and all sorts of stuff. There was one boat that came

A team of four horses and spring-toothed rake working in the valley.

past regularly that we called the 'Buttermilk Boat' because it carried a white creamy liquid. I think it used to go from the Potteries to the copper works at Froghall and the liquid was used for machining or some process.

My mother told me that in the 1920s the cut was frozen over for weeks on end and they couldn't get the slack to the pumping station at Stockton Brook to fire the engines, so that's when they built the bridge over the cut to allow the slack to be transported by road.

Children always used to swim in the cut by the pumping station as the water was always warm around there, probably heat from the boilers I should think.

There was a small wharf by Engine Lock where barges were repaired and it was run by a man named Jackson - he always seemed busy doing repairs to the passing barges.

Along the cut side up by Heakley Farm, there used to be sand banks, but they had to stop quarrying it because oil started coming up into the sand and this made it no use for anything. I believe half of Smallthorne was built using the sand from Norton Green.

I did most of my schooling at Norton until I was 11, then I had to go to Bradley school, but my mother managed to get me in at Norton Green School nearer the end because it was closer to home, so I finished my education there and left at 14. When I left I wanted to go into farming like my brother but my mother said that they'd put on me and so I started work at Bullers. The good thing was it was only a 20 minute walk along the cut side.

My brother Jack worked at Norton Hall Farm, in those days a big farm of about 200 acres with all the mowing, ploughing and carting done by shire horse. Jack was good with horses. One time they had a horse that they couldn't do anything with, so my brother put a crust in his pocket and the horse would follow him anywhere even without a halter. Jack was a bit of a lad and had a saying, 'more rain more rest', but if his bosses asked what he'd said he'd reply 'more rain more grass'. In the mowing season they would start work with the horses at 4 in the morning and work until the sun got high and then stop, then start work again in late afternoon when it had cooled down.

Other families rented land in the valley and did a bit of farming as well as doing a full day's work down the pits or on a factory. I remember the Johnson's down by Engine Lock who rented some land from Norton Hall Farm; Mr Johnson in summer would mow an acre of land by hand with a scythe before he would go to work when he was on a noon shift.

The valley wasn't as marshy in those days, as farmers would regularly clean out the ditches in the fields to drain off the water, but they do not know what a shovel is these days. That's the way things stayed in farming around here until 1941 when Joe Boulton of Yew Tree Farm bought the first tractor in the area, a Fordson Standard, and from then on horses were slowly phased out.

In 1941 I bought Cockshead Villa Farm, at this time I was paying £1 a month rent from a chap who had bought the farm from the sale of Lord Norton's Estate. Later I brought about 11½ acres of surrounding land from Beswick's to do a bit of farming.

I had carried on working at Bullers until the outbreak of the Second World War and then I was conscripted into the Army at the age of 20. I first joined the North Staffordshire Regiment but later I was transferred to the Black Watch and then the Argyles. When we were on guard duty in Germany we had to wear a kilt and sometimes the women who were passing would lift up their skirts and hope that we'd do the same! But we daren't, not when we were on duty. I often wish I'd had my photograph taken in regimental dress wearing my kilt.

I saw a lot of action in my years in the Army, fighting in France, Holland, South Africa and Germany and got injured many times with shrapnel. I also caught malaria and one time

Harry Lovatt (right)
serving in South
Africa in World
War II.

Harry in uniform

I had to be flown home in a helicopter from France with a bout of malaria.

The pay when I joined was 2 shillings a day and 4 shillings when I was demobbed. I fought in the invasion of Sicily from North Africa on 10th July 1943. After, we returned home to do our training to get ready for the 'D Day' Landings. We trained at London, Lowestoft and Great Yarmouth but we were not part of the invasion forces in the end. It was a few days later when we were sent to fight in Normandy, I think it was the 10th June.

I can remember one night in France when we were dug in and the Germans were shelling us with 'moaning minnies' as we called them, long shells like a piece of drain pipe that made a noise like a pig squealing when they were falling. Anyway in our regiment was a young chap named Charlie Walsh and he said to us that if he got injured he hoped it wasn't his hands, so he could make his living when he got home. Well I got injured with some shrapnel in my back and had to be come back to England to recuperate. When I returned to Europe I inquired about Charlie and was informed that one of these 'moaning minnies' had killed him!

After the conflict had ended I was lucky to be demobbed early as my occupation at Bullers was classed 'Class B' essential work, although by then all the celebrations and victory parties were over.

Village victory celebrations.

I continued to work at Bullers and met my future wife there, Jessie Carp from Little Heakley Farm and was married in 1956. Around 1200 people worked at Bullers at this time and there came buses from Leek, Hanley, Norton and Ball Green full of workers.

I also did a bit of farming to make my wages up and had around 200 hens. I took a lot of eggs to work to sell to other workers. One time we had a new boss at Bullers who wanted me to push carts of clay around without using the

Harry Lovatt with workmates at Bullers.

lifts to get to the other levels of the works and he said to me 'Come on Harry you must be used to carting heavy barrows of muck about', and I replied 'Yes I am, but that's for Harry and not for Bullers!'

In the sixties there were a lot of redundancies but I managed to keep my job until my retirement at Christmas 1982. If I'd worked there another month I would have been there for 49 years counting war service!

Foundry Square victory party 1945. 'When I returned home, all the celebrations and victory parties were over'.

Norton Green School

The first schooling in the village was at the Zion Methodist's Chapel on Endon Road and was a Sunday school. The teaching at Sunday school was usually run by preachers of the chapel who taught mainly religious and moral instruction to the children for a few hours a week. Rudimentary as it was it gave many children of the village their first education and was one of the fore-runners of modern state education.

In 1874 the Sunday school room was let to a Miss Hannah Beardmore for a day school at the cost of £1, for a trial period of 3 months. In August 1875 the room was let to a Miss Emma Basnett with the same charge and trial period.

The country was changing fast at this period and working people began to demand more rights, better living standards and more say in decisions that affected their lives. After much campaigning the government in 1867 passed the Reform Act which gave all male householders living in Borough constituencies the right to vote at all elections. Politicians now became increasingly concerned that if the right to vote was available to the masses, then they should be educated. Indeed the Chancellor of the Exchequer, Robert Lowe, in an address to the Houses of Parliament said 'now we have to educate our masters'.

This led to the 1870 Education Act or the 'Foster Act' which gave local authorities the power to form their own School Boards. These were given the power to raise money from local rates and donations to build new schools where they were needed. The schools were allowed to charge pupils for their tuition - 'school pence' - to a maximum of 9 pence a week and this continued until free compulsory education for all was passed in 1891.

Prospective members of the Boards would stand for election and be elected not only by the males of every household but also by women who were also allowed to vote at Board elections and could also stand to become members. Very soon over 2,500 boards were set up in England and by 1874 5,000 new schools had been founded. In February 1876 the Norton-in-the-Moors School Board was elected, seven members including Mr Wood, Mr Jones, Mr Dean and Mr Walker.

In August 1876 the trustees of the Zion Methodist's Chapel agreed to let the Sunday school room to the Norton-in-the-Moors School Board for £10 a year. In September it was agreed to paint or whitewash, as required by the board, and Thomas Knott's tender of £3 was accepted for the work. Some woodwork was also required and the tender of £3 was accepted from a John Worksop.

The school consisted of a single room of about 30ft square and was heated by a single pot bellied stove in the middle of the room, with its chimney going straight up through the ceiling. A typical school day would be 9 o'clock until 12 o'clock with the children going home for a 1 to 2 hour dinner break and returning to school in the afternoon until 4 to 5 o'clock.

Lessons followed the 'three Rs' - Reading - wRiting & aRithmetic - with scripture lessons every morning. Monitors were appointed to help out with the instruction of the classes or standards as they were known. These were older children who had some previous education or showed more promise than the average child. Some monitors went on to be appointed pupil teachers by the Board and they were required to attend further teaching at night school to attain certificates in teaching and eventually after a number of years would become qualified teachers themselves. Although being a pupil teacher was a high privilege, the working day for these children, from 13 or 14 years old, was longer than most of the teachers. Many had to walk to Burslem after school to receive their further education.

Although it was mandatory for all children to attend school from 5 to 10 years of age and children aged 10 to 14 part time, it was left to the school boards to enforce this attendance, which soon gave rise to the dreaded 'school board man'! There were many reasons for poor attendance which included poverty and non-payment of school pence, illness and seasonal work. Many older children looked after the younger members of the family while their parents were at work.

The School was opened on October 9th 1876 with Miss Hannah Mountford as Headmistress. On the first day 40 children were admitted and the number grew to 69 by October 23rd. In the following year it became more obvious that the school room was woefully inadequate for the growing numbers of children and new premises were being sought.

With new properties being built in the village even greater numbers were wanting to attend the local school, and the Board decided to build a new school within the village. A plot of land fronting Leek Road (now Endon Road) was purchased from the estate of Simeon Johnson, a local farmer from Norton Green (he also sold a plot to the trustees of the Zion Methodist's Chapel to build their premises on Endon road in 1857 for the sum of £5).

The new school was designed by the Cobridge born architect George B Johnson and work began in earnest in 1878. The school was built with the usual high windows to minimize the distraction of pupils from the outside world and consisted at this time of two main classrooms and a head's office. Each room was heated by a single open coal fire in the corner and no doubt through the winter months was a cold and uninviting place.

The new school was opened by Mr Dean and Mr Lewis of the Board 20th October 1879. It soon became firmly established within the heart of the village and was soon being used for public events, meetings, celebrations and elections. The Norton-in-the-Moors Parish Council, used it for their meetings.

The school and its staff became more and more involved in village life over the years and headmasters such as Mr Hibbs and Mr Rostance were community leaders through both world wars, overseeing not only the education and welfare of the children but also educating villagers on matters of self-sufficiency and hygiene through the epidemics of influenza and diphtheria. There role in keeping 'the home fires burning' should not be forgotten, for they kept spirits high in our village with their continual enthusiasm for England to pull through the hardest of times.

Alterations and extensions were added to the building in 1880, 1888, 1904 and 1924, with a further purchase of land at the rear of the building in the 1960s to allow the addition of mobile classrooms and a playground.

During the 1980s local government began to look at small village schools within the County and a number of schools within the local area were earmarked for closure, including Norton Green. Sadly despite the valiant efforts of local parents and children to keep the school open (known at this time as Trentside Primary and Middle school), its fate was sealed and it closed its doors to local children in 1983.

The echoes of lessons within its walls and fun and laughter in the playgrounds fell silent for the first time in over 100 years. The closure of the school changed the face of village life forever. After its closure the threat of demolition lurked over the magnificent building, fortunately at the last minute it was reprieved and purchased for use as a nursing home. The

Trentside Manor Nursing Home now looks after the local elderly instead of local children.

The school no doubt left many happy memories in the hearts of those that attended and we all have stories to tell of our time within its walls.

The Zion Methodist Chapel. The village school was held here from 1874 to 1879.

Heads of school 1874-1983.

Miss H. Beardmore............	Zion Methodists Chapel.
Miss E. Basnett....................	Zion Methodists Chapel.
Miss H. Mountford...............	Zion Methodists Chapel and Norton Green Board School
Miss A Pearsall...................	Norton Green Board School
Miss H. Rowley..............	Norton Green Board School
Miss S. Docksey................	Norton Green Board School
Mr F.E Hibbs..........................	Norton Green Board School
Mr M. Ferriday.....................	Norton Green Board School
Mr W. Rostance......................	Norton Green Board School
Mrs. K. Lloyd..................	Norton Green Board School
Mr S. Davies.........................	Norton Green Board School
Mr G. Bagnall...................	Norton Green Board School

Norton Green Board School.

1890.

1890.

Norton Green School staff 1898. Back L to R: Miss Simcock, Miss Gould, Miss Stubbs, Miss Stonier.
2nd row: Miss Wright, Miss Docksey, Miss Rowley (Head), Miss Sheldon. Front: Miss Cope, Miss Coates.

1898.

Circa 1900.

Infants 1905

Circa 1900.

Circa 1900.

Boys class. Standard 6 and 7 1919.

The school choir taken at the rear of the Zion Methodist Church 1921.

1923.

Circa 1920s.

Class 2 1923.

1924.

Class 4 1924

Circa 1920s.

Mr Rostance in the school garden with the boys 1927 (Courtesy Scholastic Souvenir Ltd. Blackpool)

Sewing class c1910.

1975/6 Schools League Champions. Back row from left: Carl Gerrard, Anthony Mullock, Steven Machin, Ian Jervis, Mr Jervis, Mrs Lloyd(head mistress), Robin Storey, Andrew Ziemann, Paul Smith, Mark Heath, Ian Gibbons. Front row from left, John Bourne, Neil Simcock, Simon Edge, Mark Sherratt, Martin Norcup, Christopher Boulton, Wayne Flowers. (Courtesy Leek Post &Times)

Class 6 1901.

c1930s

Taken around 1930s. Top L to R: Ern Smith, Jim Booth, Eric Frost, Len Mathews, Arthur Baker, Tom Richards, Joe Bossons, Mr Rostance (Headmaster). 2nd row: Doris Dawson, Ruth Heath, Ivy Corbishley, May Mathews, Gladys Steel, Elsie Sutton, Marie Sutton, Gladys Hancock, Elsie Mitchell, Florie Copeland. 3rd row: Joe Gratton, Ginny Haywood, Betty Mottram, Doris Holdcroft, Nancy Gerrard, ?? Cox, Arthur Knight. 4th row Arthur Johnson, Eric Baddeley, Enoch Salt, Arthur Hammond.

c1950s

c1950s

School Play

The captured German gun at the crossroads at Norton. This gun was given to the parish in recognition of its efforts towards the war. During this time Norton Green War Savings Association (headed by Mr Frank Edward Hibbs, the headmaster at Norton Green school) amounted war savings of £3120, the equivalent in today's money of £130,000. (Courtesy Old Nortonians Society)

SCHOOL PLAYS

Julian Ziemann - Through a lad's eyes

I moved to Norton Green with my parents and my sister Maralyn when I was three years old. I started at Norton Green Infants School when I was four and the buildings were very much as they are now except for a couple of outbuildings which have been demolished. Two striking buildings which stick in my mind were the air raid shelters erected during the Second World War, one in the bottom playground and one in the top playground, both formed from the perimeter walls and topped off with a thick concrete roof. There were two outside toilet blocks, one in the lower yard for the infants and one in the top yard for the older children. I can remember some of the older lads taking great delight in trying to wee over the top of the wall and catching innocent passers by in the playground with a most unwelcome shower.

The teacher of the infants was Miss Walker, a very benign and kindly, elderly lady who was probably coming to the end of her teaching career; she had a great deal of patience with the children. The school was attended by a mixture of children from working, professional and farming families. The walls were always heavily adorned with friezes and pictures and a large map of the world. One prominent feature was a large abacus at the front of the class which we would have to stand in front of and tell Miss Walker how many beads she had moved.

The school was always very warm and welcoming with large old fashioned radiators which were very effective. I remember one lad wrapping himself around a radiator and getting his knee trapped between the fins, but fortunately the staff managed to free him before it was necessary to call the fire brigade - but I remember he was frightened at the time.

Miss Walker used to have us standing in front of charts spelling and reciting words such as 't-h-e the' or 'c-a-t cat'. We would have to read to Miss Walker at her desk on a one to one basis - I remember this was a very effective method, although I also think that the time my parents, grandparents and aunt had already spent with me meant I was already well on my way to reading before I started school.

When you left Miss Walker's class you went into Class 2 which was run by Miss Shenton who was something of a tartar. However she was quite able to give the outward appearance of kindliness when faced by a disgruntled parent; she could be quite an ogre if she took a dislike to you. There were two lads, Donald Smith and Dave Chapman, big mates, who leaving the classroom in rather a hurry, knocked over the blackboard. I recall Miss Shenton grabbing hold of them and giving them quite a whacking over the desk. I attended the school just after the war and there was a mixture of older teachers, of the Edwardian system, and younger teachers who had been through more enlightened teacher training.

I remember the visits by the school dentist Mr Bunch with a mobile dental surgery, and in the build up to his arrival there was a lot of talk creating a lot of fear. Mr Bunch was said to have a fearsome reputation and, children being children, the stories became exaggerated. One story had it that he had gripped a child's tongue instead of his tooth and ripped it out. I had more than one sleepless night in the run up to his arrival.

Mrs Heath was a dinner lady but also acted as supervisor during playtimes and one of her duties was to dispense toilet paper; it was not kept in the toilets in case it went missing. I'm not sure on what basis she portioned out the paper, but she was never very liberal in its issue. The school dinners, by and large were good but I remember with distaste the salads which would inevitably include a rather large and tough lettuce leaf and pilchards which made me want to throw up. I invariably went hungry whenever salad was on the menu.

Much of the village activity was centred on the school, the Sunday School, or the pub, the Foaming Quart. We used to look forward to the Harvest Festival and the Christmas party which was largely financed by an annual jumble sale which was held at the school. In the build up to Christmas we made paper chains and friezes depicting Christmas scenes to decorate the school. Mrs Travis, the wife of Ern Travis the local butcher, would boil a ham so that we had boiled ham sandwiches amongst other goodies to eat, and my mother, along with others, would bake minced pies and cakes for us all. Santa Claus was regularly played by a chap named Evan Sherratt who lived in one of the cottages down by the Caldon Canal.

The Harvest Festival was a grand event and parents would send in vegetables and groceries and I remember one year someone had baked a loaf of bread in the shape of loaves and fishes which made a great centrepiece for the Festival.

Me with my sister Maralyn.

I remember Mrs Baggaley who lived on Leek Road, making a huge slab of treacle toffee and Mrs Lloyd, the Headmistress, held it aloft during morning assembly and announced it was to be broken up and sold to the children at the end of the day.

The sale of poppies at Armistice was always a big thing in the school because the sacrifices made were still in the forefront of the older teachers' minds. On one occasion some of us children were parading around the playground making fascist salutes and shouting 'Zieg Heil', and being too young to realise the significance of our actions couldn't understand the teachers' outrage at our actions. On another occasion we all sat down on the playground chanting 'we're on strike' and, again, we failed to understand the outrage our actions had caused the teachers.

On the chapel anniversaries we would all be bought new clothes for when we stood on stage during the Service. After the service these clothes would be put away and kept as 'Sunday best' for Sunday School for the rest of the year. Some of the services could be a little bit 'fire and brimstone', reflecting the style of Primitive Methodism at the time.

At the time I was at school Selworthy Road had only recently been completed, Clifford Avenue was under construction by Mr Buckley, a builder who lived in Woodland Avenue, and the Council estate was under construction and referred to as 'the scheme' - some of the older residents still refer to it as this. The classroom accommodation was very sparse and there was no facility for regular P.E. lessons, although we did sometimes go across to the Tank field and have a game of cricket and we would also take part in nature walks. We made impressions of twigs in plasticine so that we could identify different species of trees.

The first male teacher was Mr Mitchell and he was the representative of the National Union of Teachers and used to receive mail addressed to 'Mr Mitchell NUT'. We wondered what 'NUT' meant after his name, perhaps an indication of his state of mind?

We had to cover our exercise books with wallpaper - some of the children were quite alarmed at the prospect because they did not have wallpaper in their houses.

They had a savings clubs where you had a Post Office book in which a teacher would mark down all the shillings and half crowns and when you'd saved £5.00 you were issued with a

Maralyn, Geoffrey, Julian and Robert about 1960

Savings Certificate and put into a different savings book.

I left Norton Green school when I was 11 years old and went to Endon High School. All in all my memories of my time at the school were very good.

We were once playing rather noisily in our backyard and Mr Beardmore who lived next door to us was pointing across the fields and telling us to 'go and play over yonder', and we didn't know where 'yonder' was, we thought it was an actual place, not a general direction.

An annual event was haymaking and I would go with my father to help George Cantrell who owned the farm behind our house. He was always very generous and he'd give me something to eat, 'get that down yer, an empty mon's woth nowt' he'd say. He used kept hens and he'd give eggs away. The problem was the eggs were left lying around under hedges for ages and you were never sure how old they were; but you smiled and accepted the eggs graciously.

He used to have Davenport's beer delivered and he'd always give my father and me a bottle of brown ale each even though I was only a youngster. He collected waste cake from the bakeries and we youngsters would spend many hours peeling the cellophane from slabs of cherry and Genoa cake; there was nothing wrong with it, it had just gone past its sell by date.

On one occasion I was on the farm and I was told to go into the house. It later transpired that Mr Cantrell's son was fetching the bull to service one of the cows and this was considered too tender a matter for my young eyes to see. What happened was that the bull knocked Mr Cantrell's son, also George, into the 'muck ruck' and young George came into the house covered in manure. He tried to clean it off himself at the kitchen sink while old Mr Cantrell was doubled up laughing.

The Cantrell's were not known for their cleanliness and they also used to fix chicken wire around the sides of the kitchen table and keep hens under the table. They rarely emptied the teapot and would just keep adding more tea leaves on top of the old tea leaves until there would be very little water in the pot, just a load of stewed old tea leaves. They had an outside privy and I remember asking once where young George was, and I was told that he was 'down the office'. I was surprised to learn that they had an office. I was pointed in the direction of the privy and I went down shouting for George and the door opened and there he was, sitting on the privy. There was an orchard with apple and pear trees at the front of the house and that's where the privy used to get emptied.

As a youngster I would accompany George on his rounds of fish and chip shops and collect all their waste food, which would be boiled up in one of two copper boilers to form pig swill. The only problem was the pigs used to taste of fish and none of the local butchers would buy them and they had to be sent to a Government organisation to process the meat that way.

On one occasion I'd called at the farm on my way from school, so I was wearing my school uniform, short trousers and long socks, and I was trying to look over into the sty to see how many pigs there were. I lost my footing and managed to step into the blocked up outflow from the sty. Mr Cantrell washed my socks in one of the two wells which were situated on the farm and he took them into the house and hung them over the grate to dry and Mrs Cantrell asked in a high pitched voice 'why doesn't he go home and put on a pair of his father's?'

School children preparing for the Harvest Festival.

Mrs Cantrell was an elderly lady and I remember her reclining on a chaise lounge. She had a great fondness for snuff which she kept in a large cocoa tin; she had a lot of brown marks from the snuff around her nose and she kept a pile of serviettes ready to hand with which to wipe her nose.

There was another local character named Sam Hancock who was a very skilled fieldsman. One day he'd caught a rabbit alive and he was walking home through Heakley Hall Farm with the rabbit in his pocket when he met the farmer Jack Clewes. The farm had a large field of cabbages and Sam asked Jack if he could have one, but this request was refused so Sam decided to repay Jack's lack of generosity by releasing the rabbit into the field of cabbages.

There used to be a rag and bone man who would call at the Foaming Quart for a pint and leave his horse and cart on the car park. On one occasion, whilst the rag and bone man was in the pub someone unhitched the cart from the horse and threaded the shafts through the gate into the field adjacent the pub car park and re-harnessed it so that the gate was between the horse and cart. When, some time later the rag and bone man left the pub he was heard to say to the horse 'well you got yourself into this, you can get yourself out of it', before he realised what had happened and set about unhitching the horse and putting things right.

The landlord of the Foaming Quart for many years was Alec Hancock who had a number of sidelines to make money. One of the things was to cut hair and on one particular occasion he'd shut the pub and was relaxing in the back room when there came a knock on the back door. He opened the door to see our next door neighbour, Lindon Evans, standing before him with a towel wrapped around his head. Lindon asked 'cos do anything with this?' and removed the towel to reveal that he'd unsuccessfully tried to cut his own hair. The only way Alec could improve things was to shave Lindon's head. Lindon, fearing his wife's wrath, then talked my father into having his head shaved too so that he could tell her that it was a local trend and that he was not the only man in the village embarrassing his family.

The School Harvest Festival.

School Christmas party.

Christmas festivities at the school with Head teacher Mrs Lloyd, Mrs Graham, Head dinner lady Mrs Sherratt and Mrs Taylor.

My brother Robert Ziemann front row second from left.

School Pantomime. A few names I remember - Heather Bailey, Julian Ziemann, John Rodgerson, Linda Sutton, Linda Cartwright.

School Pantomime. Christine Heath, Ann Clews, Sheena Gowans, John Mottram, Brian Evans, Gerald Scragg, Barry Sheldon, Janet Winkle, Irene Wooliscroft, Barbara Mould, Peter Holdcroft, Michael Graham, Trevor Mountford, Maralyn Ziemann, Lynn Stanner, Donald Cooper, Valimars Gravis, Garry Holdcroft.

School Pantomine. Jeffrey Proctor, Gwen Simpson, Jean Lowndes, Linda Holland, Sylvia Beardmore, Susan Beardmore, Peter Jackson, Dennis Holdcroft, Geoffrey Ziemann, Roger Holdcroft, Geoffrey Holdcroft.

Murder at Norton Green Hall

Norton Green Hall is one of the oldest inhabited sites in the Parish and the recorded home of the de-Mere or de Norton family as far back as the 13th century, possibly even earlier - we do not know whether earlier members of the family controlled the Manor from the site. The present Hall dates from around 1650 and replaced former halls built there.

The de Mere family roots were firmly established by then and they could trace their lineage back to the early Saxon kings of England. Domesday shows the Lordship of the Manor of 'Northune' (Norton-in-the-Moors) in the possession of Ulviet de Meiri, whose Saxon name was Wulfgeat, the name de Meiri being adopted after 1066 to show allegiance.

The most noted member of the de Mere family to live at the Hall was Sir William (1264-1324) son of Nicholas. William lived under the reign of Edward I (Longshanks) and it was probably Edward who knighted William and granted him the right to bear arms. William's wealth continued to grow and by 1290 he had become the first MP for Staffordshire. By 1305 he was Bailiff to Burton Abbey and in 1314 High Sheriff of Staffordshire.

The de Mere's association with Burton Abbey can be traced back to its formation in 1004; it was a blood relative and the former Lord of Norton, 'Wulfric Spot', Earl of Mercia and Chief counsellor to Ethelred (the Unready) who founded the Abbey. William also had connections with St Mary's in Abbey Hulton, granting the Abbey lands at Maer near Normacot in 1300.

We can imagine the Hall at this time being a grand, fortified stronghold with William's high position and wealth, his family enjoying all the pleasures befitting their status. All that would change one dreadful night in the year 1315.

The Murder of Sir William de Mere's Son 1315.

Notable families married their children to families of the same rank and Sir William's daughter Agnes was no exception marrying Sir Robert Dutton of Dutton, Cheshire. The Duttons were a notorious family who took the law into their own hands on many occasions to get what they wanted. Members of the family were not brought to account for their deeds because Cheshire at this time was not subject to the laws of the land (Palatinate of Chester).

Upon his marriage Sir Robert was given land by his mother Phillippa within the close proximity of Norton and soon the Manor held by his father in law became a very interesting prospect. There was one major obstacle that stood in the way of Sir Robert inheriting the Norton Manor through his marriage; Agnes had a brother. For the estate to come into Sir Robert's hands, William's son needed to be taken out of the equation by natural means or foul.

The prospect manifested itself into murderous intent and members of the Dutton family raised a mob to ride to Norton Green Hall to slay the father and son. On their arrival at the Hall a fight ensued between the mob from Cheshire and the defenders of the Hall. Amidst the mayhem Sir William escaped but his son was butchered.

Whether or not the Dutton's were held accountable for this crime we have not discovered but having no intention of granting his lands and title to his daughter and her murderer husband, Sir William 'enfeoffed' (willed) his estate to the Lords of Stafford and Audley.

This murder at the Hall may account for a local story relating to the lane that runs to the rear of the Old Hall. It is known as 'Hacker's' or 'Akers Lane' and people believe it got its name from a member of the household at the Hall who was killed there with an axe! Was this then where Sir William's son met his untimely death?

Muriel Lancaster - Memories of my mother

Edith Cope, my mother, was born in 1885 at 12 Trent Terrace (formerly Brook Terrace), Norton Green, the only daughter of John and Ann Cope. She had three brothers, John William who died at six, Bernard and George. They were direct descendants of the Cope family of engineers who owned the Iron Foundry in Foundry Square. John's brother,James, lived at 10 Trent Terrace.

Edith attended Norton Green School along with her three brothers. At the age of 13, the leaving age at that time, she became a pupil teacher. This meant helping a teacher in the classroom all day, then, two or three nights a week, walking to Burslem to the Wedgwood Institute in Queen Street to study Arithmetic, English, History, Geography, etc. It took five years to train and she was paid about three shillings a week. Pupil teachers' work was closely watched by teachers and inspectors and if they did well, they would become qualified teachers when they were 18. So, at the age of 18, Edith joined the staff at Norton Green School.

These are some of the things she told me about school life at that time:
The children sat in rows of desks with the teacher at the front and were not allowed to leave their desks without permission. The teachers were very strict. Children had to behave well all the time and there were harsh punishments for children who did not obey their teacher.

They all learnt the alphabet and to make lists of words from the letters and so learnt to read. As paper was expensive, they copied on to a slate with a slate pencil. This could be wiped clean and used over and over again. Some slates were marked with lines so children could learn to write straight and keep all their letters the same size. Older children wrote on paper with pen and ink. A boy or girl called the ink monitor was responsible for pouring blue or black ink into the ink wells on the desks. It was hard not to blot work when first learning to write with pen and ink. They had a copy book so that they could learn copperplate handwriting. The sentence was written at the top of each page and was copied many times on to the blank lines underneath. Sometimes the teacher read from a book for the children to write down - dictation.

Children had to know their multiplication tables thoroughly, which they learnt by reciting in chorus with their teacher. They also learnt historical and geographical facts in this way. Arithmetic was a very important subject. The youngest children used ball frames with coloured beads to learn how to add and take away. Older children had to learn to do sums in their head - mental arithmetic - and sums with money. They used imperial measures then - pounds, shillings and pence, ounces, pounds and hundredweights, pints, quarts, gallons, pecks and bushels, yards, feet and inches. By the age of 13, most children could do quite long and difficult sums.

P.E. was not very exciting. The children stood in long lines in the playground and did exercises copying their teacher who stood at the front. At playtime, the children played hopscotch, marbles, tiddlywinks and skipping. The boys played with iron hoops which could be rolled round the playground with a stick. Every day began with prayers and religious instruction.

Inspectors visited the school from time to time and the first thing they did was to count the children, then check the register. Registers had to be kept very thoroughly, including notes on punctuality and comments on behaviour. The inspector would then test the children on tables, mental arithmetic, reading and handwriting. If a child was absent, the School Board man would visit the home. School in those days was hard work - it was not meant to be fun!

I, myself, joined the staff at Norton Green School in January 1967 and taught there until its closure in 1983, a very sad day for the village.

John Cope, my grandfather a descendent of the Copes of Norton Green Foundry.

Ann Cope, my grandmother.

John and Ann Cope at the rear of number 12 Trent Terrace (formerly called Brook Terrace).

My mother Edith Cope born 1885 a teacher at Norton Green school.

Trent Terrace formerly Brook Terrace, and the infant River Trent.

Teachers of Norton Green Board School 1901: Back row L to R: Miss Gaskell, Miss Docksey. Middle: Miss Sheldon, Miss Sarah Docksey (Headmistress), Miss Wright.
Front:Miss Edith Cope, Miss Coates, Miss Stonier.

Staff and pupils at the closure of the school in 1983. 'A very sad day for the village'.

Senior Citizens' Christmas Lunch at Trentside School.

Mrs Lloyd the former headmistress of Norton Green School being presented
with a bouquet of flowers at the closure in 1983.

Norman Holdcroft - Reflections of my time at the Church

I was baptised as a baby but my first real time at the church was Sunday School in 1936. Sunday School in those days was both morning and afternoon. There were around 50 children then and I have many memories of Sunday School outings and of being on the stage at Anniversary time and taking part in concerts.

In the Second World War the men at the Chapel had to make shutters for the windows to comply with 'Black Out' regulations so that evening meetings could take place. On the evening of V.E. Day, the day the war in Europe ended, a thanksgiving service was held and likewise on V.J. Day when war with Japan ended.

On 12th May 1947 I was one of a group of young people who were received into membership of the Church. At the end of 1947 I was called up for National Service, spent mainly in Germany. When I was demobilized at the end of 1949, I picked up the threads of work at the Chapel.

My wife and I first met in the Schoolroom of the Chapel, we were married there in 1951 and have since then both worked there in various positions. Both our boys were baptised there.

In 1952 I began to study to become a Methodist Preacher and I was received as an accredited preacher in 1957. During the years I have seen many changes take place but I've been glad the Chapel has been there to witness to the village. In 1957 the Chapel celebrated its Centenary, and now in 2007 we have celebrated 150 years of Christian witness here.

The Zion chapel looking down Leek Road (now Endon Road).

Norton Green Foundry

Foundry Square, as the name suggests, derives is origins from its industrial past when the village had a thriving iron foundry using natural resources readily available in the valley. Many residents have commented on the foundry and its supply of chains for the Menai Suspension Bridge.

During the 1780s George Cope built an iron foundry on the canal side at Milton next to the mill of his father-in-law William Sherratt, an engineer and part owner of Cockshead Colliery at Norton Green. George's business grew and flourished picking up many contracts in the vicinity through William Sherratt's business dealings.

A cousin of George Cope, Thomas Cope, set up business at Norton Green, having secured a lease from the then Lord Norton, Charles Bowyer Adderley. The business was started in 1815 as Thomas Cope and Sons, civil engineers, boiler makers and iron founders.

The foundry had two furnaces and boilers situated behind Foundry House. Many buildings in the square, now long gone, such as Foundry Farm, were part of the works.

Natural resources were close at hand and his business flourished and became a major employer in the village. Coal from the Cockshead and Froggery mines along with many other drift mines in the village were used to feed the hungry furnaces and boilers, along with sand from Heakley for mould castings. With the canal arm of the Caldon coming virtually into the works transport was not a problem.

Many large and ambitious engineering projects were in progress at this time, none more so than the construction of Thomas Telford's suspension bridge at Menai, the first of its type in the world. Work began in 1819 and the contract for the iron work going to Mr Hazeldine, to cast the iron links in Upton Magna, Shropshire. To make the sixteen huge chains for the 579 foot span, 33,264 large links were required. It is plausible that this amount would be too much for any single foundry and that some of the work was contracted out to other foundries. This is unconfirmed but Thomas Cope could well have picked up a part contract for the supply of links.

By 1836 Thomas Cope had died and the business was run by a partnership of his three sons, Thomas (b.1799. d.1852), George (b.1805. d. 1861) and John (b. 1802. d. 1852) who was head of the company. The business went from strength to strength and Whites Directory 1851 states *'there is a large iron foundry lying in Norton Green'*.

By 1852 John Cope had died and his son Charles (b.1832) was principal owner of the foundry. Around this time construction began on the row of cottages on the west side of Foundry Square (Nos 2-16, 18 and 20 added c.1871) known locally as 'Yellow Row'. Charles Cope probably financed this, but whether the properties were initially to house the workers of the foundry, or just a financial venture is not sure. The 1861 Census shows properties rented to residents of varying occupations:

No 2.	James Unwin. - Grocer and Master Baker.
No 4.	John Simcock. - Iron Moulder.
No 6.	Joseph Mountford. - Iron Moulder.
No 8.	Reuben Sant. - Joiner.
No 10.	Edward Marsh. - Pattern Maker.
No. 12.	Theodosia Lancaster. - Mangle Woman.
No. 14.	Joseph Holdcroft. - Coal Miner.
No. 16.	Thomas Docksey. - Iron Moulder.

The census also says that the large iron foundry employs 27 men and 4 boys.

The name 'Yellow Row' we surmise came from the fact that the front elevation of the properties was built of yellow brick, but a number of our residents have recalled that their parents told them that the name came about because the residents in the row worked in the foundry and had yellow tainted skin. It is easy to dismiss this as an old wives' tale but maybe there is some truth in this explanation.

By 1869 a new partnership had been formed, with trade directories advertising the business as Barker and Cope, Iron Founders, Norton Green. In 1871 the business ceased to operate in the village and the partnership moved to the Union Foundry at Kidsgrove, operating as Barker and Cope, General Engineers.

After 1880 the Cope family's long association with iron foundries comes to an end when the works at Kidsgrove were acquired by a new partnership of King and Renshaw. Recent research has revealed an 1864 agreement for the lease of lands signed between the Chesterton Estate and Thomas Eaton, Sam Dale, Henry Sherratt, George Barker and Charles Cope acting as the Chesterton Mining Company. So perhaps Charles Cope's engineering skills were now engaged in the extraction of coal.

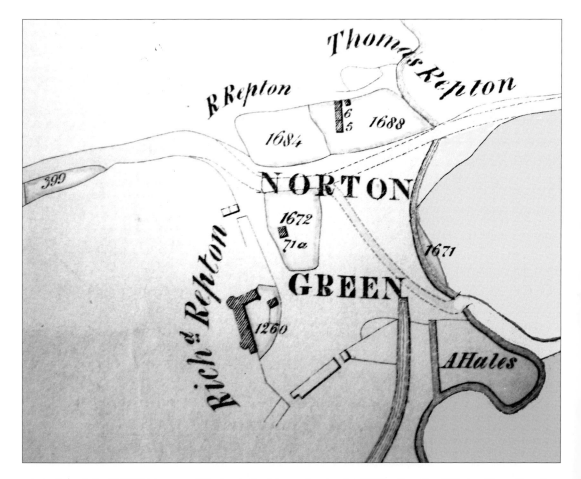

A section of the 1840 Estate map of Norton in the Moors showing lot 1260 as the site of Norton Green Foundry.

Stephanie Mountford - Happy days in Happy Valley

Living in our village has been a brilliant life. My parents, Cynthia and Pawell Ziemann moved into 132 Leek Road in February 1954 along with my eldest brother Julian and elder sister Maralyn. My parents later had four more children, Geoffrey, Robert, me and our youngest brother Andrew. My father was Polish and came to England after the Second World War and he lived for a short time at Blackshaw Moor Camp.

I was born in the front room of my parents' terraced house in March 1961 and had a really happy childhood. I went to Norton Green Infants and Junior School. The Head teacher was Mrs Lloyd, and other teachers included Mrs Taylor, Mrs Dean, Mrs Colclough, Mrs Holdcroft, Mrs Foden, Mrs Lancaster, Mrs Graham, Mr Boothenstone, Mr Grimley, Mrs Bedson and Mrs Dawson. While I was there two mobile classrooms were added and a mobile dinner hall where every morning we would gather for Assembly and say 'Good morning Mrs Lloyd, good morning teachers and good morning everybody', sing hymns and say prayers before going back to our classrooms.

Most of the children in the village, like me, came from big families. We were poor but very happy and there was a great community spirit because everyone knew each other and everybody would help each other out if they could. The Methodist Chapel also played an important part of growing up in the village because, as children, we were all encouraged to attend Sunday School every week. I remember when I was only four or five years old, we would sit on our chairs and at the end of the line was a collection plate and we would walk around the line of chairs singing: 'Dropping, dropping, Hear the pennies fall, Everyone for Jesus, He shall have them all.' I just loved singing that song so much that when I got home I would have my mum and dad and all my siblings sitting in a row while I walked around

Members of my family playing by the 'Ringle'.

them with my father's cap having them dropping pennies in while I sang the collection song, unaware that they weren't taking it as seriously as me and had to control their fits of laughter.

I remember some of my Sunday School teachers, Mr Norman Holdcroft, Mr Mountford and the organist Mrs Bertha Hancock. Every year when it was the Chapel Anniversary we would wear white dresses, socks and sandals and sing in front of our parents on the stage. I was in the retinue for three years for the crowning of the Sunday School Queen and Janet Brown was my Retinue Queen. We also used to have pantomimes at the chapel and everyone would turn out to watch the children doing their act.

Because we were poor, we played together and in summer our mums would make jam butties and orange cordial and we would go across the fields at the back of Yardley Street for the day. We would go to the 'Ringle' in our swimming costumes where we would paddle and there was a small clay bank there where you could use your fingers to rip out bits of clay and make little men or ashtrays, then leave them to dry in the sun and take them home to your mums at the end of the day.

> Over the iron bridge we'd go,
> To the Ringle where the waters flow,
> With its banks smooth with clay,
> For hours at potters we'd play,
> Our wares would dry beneath the sun,
> Then carry our trophies home to mum,
> Then tea, and off to bed to dream,
> Of playing in the Ringle stream.

We would dare each other to do 'doffers' across the brook; you would find a wide part of the brook and jump from one side to the other without falling in. A lot of the time we would all land in the water and we would run around the fields whirling our socks around to get them dry so that our mums wouldn't find out. Once when I was always coming home filthy from head to toe, and as we had no bathroom it was hard work for my mum to keep getting the big tin bath out, she threatened to stand me in the yard with nothing on in a bowl of warm soapy water and scrub me with the yard brush if I didn't stop getting 'made away' with mud. As I didn't think she was serious I took no notice and, as you can probably guess, my mum stuck to her word and I learned the hard way as she carried out her threat.

As well as playing the usual games like skipping, hide and seek, ball tick and kiss chase with the boys we would also make our own carts with wheels from unwanted prams and pushchairs and race each other. When it was haymaking time children used to help the local farmers collect the hay bales, and it was a great time. My brother Andrew and I were friends with David and Stephen Machin who lived at Yew Tree Farm with their parents Colin and Joyce and we would help to collect the eggs from the hens and when it was milking time we would sometimes be allowed to help weigh the corn to feed the cows while they were being milked. Occasionally we would have a drink of milk that had come straight from the cow and was still warm. You wouldn't be allowed to do that today!

By the end of the 1960s most people had got outside flushing toilets or, if you were lucky, an inside bathroom, but there were still a few old properties with the old 'earth closets' and the 'muck man' would have to come and empty them. The stench was horrible and it always seemed to be around mid-day, just as you were having your dinner, when they were emptied so mum would shut the doors and windows to try to stop the smell from coming into the house. I always remember when we used to play up Back Lane that runs behind Lime Kiln Cottages and Bill and Anna Baddeley, an elderly couple who lived in one of the cottages, still had an old earth closet and every week Bill would fill the buckets himself and leave them outside their yard for the muck man to collect. When we walked past, the smell would make us feel sick but at the same time we found it hilarious that people still had these old toilets.

Bonfire Night was a great time of year. There used to be two bonfires built in the village, one on the Tankfield that the kids from the Council Estate built and one on some spare ground behind Yardley Street that the kids from the other end of the village built and there was always competition between us to build the best bonfire. The children used to collect the wood over the weeks leading up to Bonfire Night and, on the day, our dads would help to build the bonfire up and in the evening when the fireworks were set off our mums would bring us soup or let us cook jacket potatoes in the embers of the fire.

One year we built our bonfire in the garden of our neighbours Bill and Vera Biddulph. Mr Biddulph had got rid of his hens and was burning the old sheds and my brother Geoffrey and two of his mates were letting off fireworks. He had a firework called a Jumping Jack which would jump around making a loud noise. Being the little devil he was, my brother got an old tin bath, lit a Jumping Jack and covered it with the upturned bath and dared me to sit on the bath. He burst into fits of laughter at me, terrified and crying and not daring to move with this Jumping Jack battering the inside of the tin bath.

Apart from our 'Sunday best' clothes which we had to change out of after Sunday School, we could not afford new clothes like they do today, so everyone used to look forward to both the school and the chapel's regular jumble sales. These used to be great events where people with large families kitted their kids out cheaply and we would be thrilled to bits to get a good choice of 'cast offs' or cheap secondhand toys. It was one of the many highlights of village life because everyone was in the same boat.

Because we could not afford holidays one of the exciting times of the year was the Sunday School trips to Rhyl or Blackpool and, if your parents were members of Brown Edge or Norton Workingmen's Clubs you also got to go on the Workingmen's Club trip. The exciting thing about the club trip was that you were given crisps and pop to eat and drink on the coach and when you got to your destination you were given ten bob in a little brown envelope to spend on yourself.

A lot of the social aspect of people's lives was down to the choice of little shops that we had. Your parents would always be nattering and catching up with local gossip while doing their weekly or daily shopping. The hairdressers or the Foaming Quart were other places where people would meet up. We used to have a local Post Office cum greengrocers which belonged to Mr and Mrs Mottram, a decorating shop owned by Mrs Walley, Mrs Potts had a toffee/food shop, Des and Betty Sheldon ran the chip shop, Mr and Mrs Sherratt owned the newsagents and I would occasionally help out in Mr and Mrs Clewes shop where they sold loose biscuits from square tubs. Grace and Anne Chadwick ran the hairdressers shop next door but one to my parents' house and their parents, Mr and Mrs Chadwick, owned the greengrocery at the end of Mayer Street, (now Frobisher Street). There was also the butchers on Endon Road run by Amy Travis and her son and his wife, John and Jean. Reg Simpson from Old Hall Farm used to sell vegetables from his horse and cart on Saturdays.

By the mid-1970s most of these shops started to disappear, either because their owners retired or passed away but also because Norton Co-op had been built and other supermarkets started to spring up in the towns which took trade away from the local shops. Even the school closed down due to the lack of children in the village. My mother used to joke with me that it was my generation's fault for not having big families - all I can say is thank goodness for television, the great contraceptive of the modern age!

But even though these amenities are long gone, we still have a beautiful village and hopefully people who are new to Norton Green will grasp what village life was really like and hopefully, through the Residents' Association, keep that community spirit alive.

Stephanie in her retinue dress.

Limekiln Cottage. Bill and Anna Baddeley's house.

My brother Robert Ziemann
Endon Road early 1960s

My dad Pawel (Paul) and brother Andrew Ziemann with my
Uncle Tom on Endon Road in the late 1960s.

Norton Green Chapel Queen and retinue early 1960s. My brother Geoff Ziemann third from left.

Norton Green late 1980s taken from Back Lane.

A Brief History of the Zion Methodist Church

Early in the 19th Century there was no church in Norton Green and the first Primitive Methodist Society met in an old preaching house which has now gone. It was the end cottage by the entrance to Back Fold Farm, and here Hugh Bourne, one of the founders of Primitive Methodism preached his last sermon on 22nd January 1852. He died 11th October 1852. Meetings were also held at the foundry works of Mr Cope.

In 1857 a plot of land was purchased from Simeon Johnson a local farmer and member of the Primitive Methodist Connexion for the sum of £5.00 for the erection of the first Chapel, a rectangular, one roomed, single storey building, this being the present schoolroom. The date stone on the front gable declares:

Primitive Methodist

1857

Prepare to meet thy God

Amos Ch.4: V12

This building was furnished with simple wooden benches and heated by a stove pot, the flue pipe going straight up through the roof. The cost of the building was £285.00, and the builder named Chadwick. It was to serve the congregation for the next fourteen years.

As the ranks of the Society increased, another building was needed and in 1871 a plot of land next to the first chapel was purchased for £37-1s-0d, and the present chapel was erected. The front gable was inscribed:

Zion Primitive Methodist

1871

This building was larger and the seating capacity further increased by the inclusion of a gallery which was removed in 1985. Again the heating was a stove pot. The first building became the Sunday School and also from 1874 to 1879 it was used as the Village Day School until the Norton Green Board School was built in 1879.

Norton Green was noted for holding Camp Meeting services on the Village Green. The first one is believed to have been on 23rd August 1807, following the very first Mow Cop Camp meeting. The Norton Green one was known as the 'Crucial Camp Meeting' because it led to Hugh Bourne being excluded from the Wesleyan Methodist Church. As a result, along with a potter called William Clowes and others, he formed the Primitive Methodist Church.

In 1881 Zion agreed to hold a Camp Meeting on Norton Wakes Sunday. From that date Camp Meetings were held each year until 1966 when the older members of the church felt they could no longer worship in the open air.

In May 1919 a pedal organ was purchased and placed in the Chapel as a memorial to those who had died in the Great War 1914-1918. Over the years there have been three organs put in and each one counted as a memorial to those who died in both wars. Added to this in 2006 the Village Residents Association placed a brass plaque in memory of those who died in the 1914-18 war, along with a Book of Remembrance and poppy wreath at the Remembrance Service. After further research another plaque will go in place in 2007, on Remembrance Sunday, 11th November.

The church premises were refurbished in 1999 in time to meet the new millennium and 2007 marks the 150th Anniversary of the Zion Methodist Church, Norton Green.

1950 Rev. Arthur Newman, William Dawson and Barbara Yardley.

Early chapel queen

Early chapel queen

Norton Green Sunday School queen, Patricia Holdcroft

The first Garden Party, which was held in the field by the Chapel 8th August 1942.
The Sunday School Queen was Margaret Shufflebotham.

'A Ladies Day' Chapel outing.

Chapel Queen and retinue, Margaret Shufflebotham, Dorothy Heath and Wendy Fisher.

The former meeting house (now demolished) at Foundry Square where Hugh Bourne preached his last sermon.

On the chapel steps. Anna Mayer, Lizzie Holdcroft, Annie Heath, Miriam Lawton, Mrs Hamblet (mother of Lol Hamblet of Port Vale fame), Mrs Barber, Rev. J Roberts, Joe Mayer, Bill Dawson, Ann White.

Chapel queen, Dorothy Heath. From left, Bill Dawson, Alan Buckley, Amos Mayer, Roger Wright, Bill Dawson (Senr), George Barber, Rev. Arthur Wilkes, Bill Simcock, Arthur Baddeley.

The ladies of the Zion Methodist Chapel.

LEFT.
July 1959, Sunday School
Queen Dianne Lawton with
Rev W.J. Atkinson and Mrs
Peggy Grimley, the crowner.

BELOW.
September 1973, Sunday School Queens
Lynne Sherratt and Jane Bryan.

Chapel outing probably in the 1920s.

Sunday School Queen, Maureen Newman, 1951.

The old organ in the Zion Methodist Church.